Learn to Play Chess

Learn to Play Chess

35 easy and fun chess activities for children aged 7 years +

Jessica E. Martin   CICO kidz

For my sweet Baby Albert, my absolute joy.
And for all children, girls and boys, who want to
play chess: you can do it, and don't give up!

This edition published in 2021 by CICO Kidz
An imprint of Ryland Peters & Small
20–21 Jockey's Fields   341 E 116th St
London WC1R 4BW   New York, NY 10029
www.rylandpeters.com

First published in 2014 as *My First Chess Book*

10 9 8 7 6 5 4 3 2 1

Text © Jessica E. Martin 2014
Design, illustration, and photography
© CICO Kidz 2014

A CIP catalog record for this book is available from
the Library of Congress and the British Library.

ISBN: 978 1 80065 057 2

Printed in China

Editor: Robin Gurdon
Designer: Barbara Zuñiga
Photographer: Penny Wincer
Stylist: Isabel de Cordova
Animal artworks: Hannah George
Step artworks: Rachel Boulton
Art director: Sally Powell
Head of production: Patricia Harrington
Publishing manager: Penny Craig
Publisher: Cindy Richards

Contents

Introduction

Chess is fun and universal! You can play with your friends and family, with anyone of any age, all over the world! It's also much easier to get started than you'd imagine as you really only have to learn how to move six different pieces. Once you've got the hang of that, there are lots of exciting activities to master, each of which will make you a better chess player!

Every activity in this book has a skill level of one, two, or three (see below) so you can tell when you're ready to try each one. There is also a helpful glossary on page 13, which explains special chess terms that are used throughout the activities.

You can learn a lot with this book, and end up beating your dad or mom quite soon! Sometimes you will win and sometimes you will lose, but remember always to be a good sport, and bow or shake hands with your partner when the game is over.

Activity skill levels

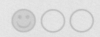

Level 1

These are quick and simple activities for new players.

Level 2

You will need to have mastered Level 1 activities before you try these, but they are easy once you've done that.

Level 3

Trophy level! These activities are more challenging and you may want to ask an adult to help you with them.

The Materials

What do you need to play a chess game? Really very little: all you require is a chess set, which includes a board and pieces. Plus, though you could play by yourself, it's usually more exciting to play against a friend!

Your board could have numbers and letters on it (see page 8), or be blank around the edges. It could be made of wood or marble or glass, but the easiest (and safest!) board to carry around is simply made of vinyl or cloth. Similarly, the pieces could be made of any kind of material. You can even create your own set out of clay or papier-mâché! It doesn't even matter what color the pieces are as long as the two sides are different. I've seen red and blue, pink and black…you could choose your favorite colors!

Naming the Squares

Let's take a look at our board first. There are 64 squares on a chessboard. Each square has a name—a first and a last name, just like you and me! It's very easy to remember all these squares' names, because their first name is the letter below, and their last name is the number to the side. We say the letter first, then the number. So the first square's name is a1. (In chess, we don't capitalize the squares' names.)

What if you move up a square? This square's first name is still a, but now its last name is 2. So its full name is a2. What about the one above that? It's a3! I'm sure you can figure out all the squares' names just by looking at the letters and numbers! Try it—point to any square on the board and say its name.

The horizontal and vertical rows also have names. The horizontal rows are called ranks, while the vertical rows (or columns) are called files. So, for example, we would call row number two the "second rank," and we would call the column labeled c the "c-file."

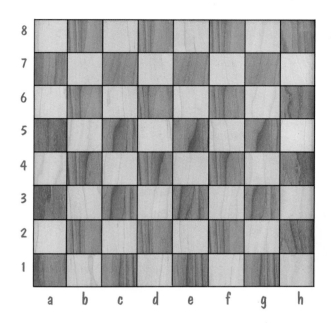

Setting up the Board

As you're looking at the board, whether you're playing as White or Black, the white square always goes on the right-hand side. ("White" and "right" rhyme, so it should be easy to remember that one!)

If your board has letters and numbers on it, remember that a1 is always on the same side as White—it'll be the bottom left square. (So if you are playing as Black, the bottom left square from your viewpoint is always h8.) Now you need to find out where the pieces go!

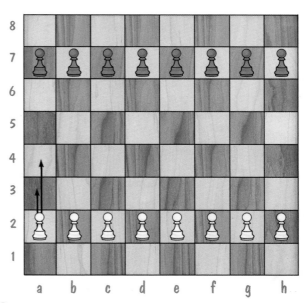

The Chess Pieces

Now let's take a look at our chess pieces. There are six pieces in chess: each one has its own starting position on the board and has its own way of moving around. A chess piece can capture other pieces by moving onto the square of the piece they want to capture, then removing their opponent's piece from the board. Unlike in checkers (draughts), which you might have played, most chess pieces cannot jump over other pieces—only one piece, the knight, can do this. Chess pieces need a clear route to move along.

Pawns

Pawns

First, we have the pawns—little guys! There are always eight pawns in chess that stand in front of your bigger pieces to start. Some people think of them as soldiers. Pawns have four rules:

1. Pawns can only move forward.

2. Pawns always capture one square diagonally forward.

3. Pawns can move either one or two squares on their first move, but only one square on each move after that.

4. When a pawn gets to the other side of the board, it can promote to a queen, rook, bishop, or knight. ("Promote" means it gets changed into one of these more powerful pieces.)

Because pawns can only move forward if they're not capturing another piece, pawns that are head to head are frozen and cannot move. They have to wait for another piece to come along that they can capture diagonally!

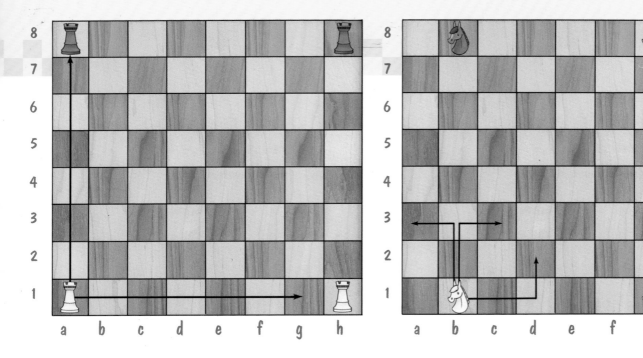

Rooks

Here are the rooks. They always start in the corners of your board. They look like towers or castles. In fact, some people use the word castle for rook, but that's not really accurate, because castling is the name of a special move we'll learn about later, not a chess piece.

Rooks can move forward, backward, or sideways, as many squares as they want, but cannot jump over other pieces.

Knights

Next square in go the knights. These are shaped like horses in most chess sets but they are called knights, because knights used to ride horses into battle.

Knights are very special pieces because they are the only ones that jump over other pieces. They move in an L-shape, always going "one, two, turn." They can move forward or backward, as long as they move in an L-shape.

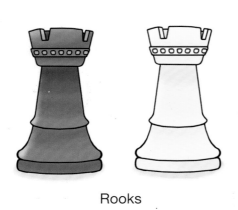

Rooks

Knights

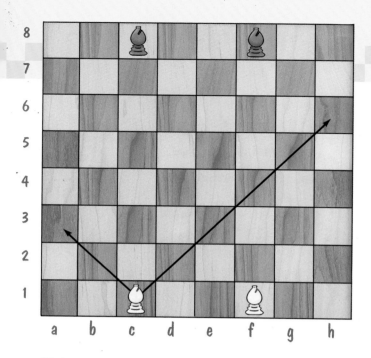

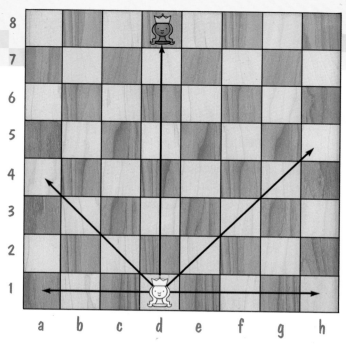

Bishops

Next to the knights go the bishops. Bishops used to be called elephants, and still are in some countries today. Bishops will always have that little slit in their hats so they look like they are frowning. Turn them upside down to see them smile!

Notice how they are placed on opposite colors. Bishops must always stay on their starting color and they can only move diagonally, but they can move forward or backward on the diagonal line. They cannot jump over other pieces.

Queens

The queen and king are placed in the center of the first rank. You can always remember how to set them up, because the queen goes on her color. Light queen, light square; dark queen, dark square. Some people think of the queen as wearing shoes to match her dress. The queens will always be opposite each other along the d-file!

Queens can move like both rooks and bishops: forward, backward, side to side, and diagonally as far as they like, but they cannot jump over other pieces.

Bishops

Queens

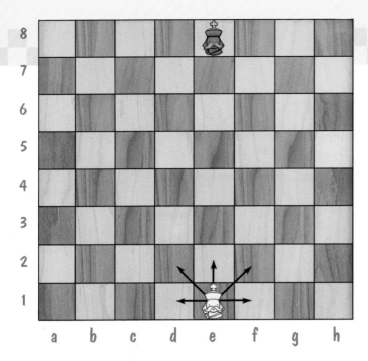

Kings

The king is placed next to the queen. He can also move in any direction, but only one square at a time. The most important rule to learn about the king is that he can never be captured—it just isn't allowed! You'll learn more about this in Opposing Kings (see page 35).

Kings

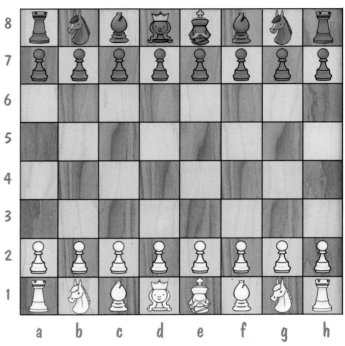

Playing a Game

Set up your board and place all your pieces in their starting positions—then you're ready to go! White always goes first, and then you take turns.

During the game you are trying to do lots of things, including capturing the other player's pieces while also protecting your own and getting your pawns to the other side (see page 9), but the ultimate goal of the game is to trap the other side's king in something called **checkmate**. This is when the king is completely unable to escape. We'll talk a lot more about this word later, but remember— you are never allowed to capture the king! However, before you play a full game of chess, try out the activities in this book to help you practice the moves and learn tons of tricks to help you win.

Chess Terms

Absolute pin—a pin where the king is at the back, so the middle piece cannot move (because doing so would put the king in **check**, which is not allowed)

Castling—a strategy to keep the king safe, using the king and rook (see page 50)

Castling short—castling kingside

Castling long— castling queenside

Center—the middle of the board—squares d4, d5, e4, and e5

Check—the king is in danger and you must move, block, or capture to escape (see page 40)

Checkmate—game over; the king cannot escape from check; one side wins and the other loses

Chess clock—a special double clock that times how long you take to play (see page 63)

Develop—bring pieces out from their home squares

Discovered attack— three pieces are in a line and when the middle piece moves, the piece behind makes the attack (see page 90)

Double attack—one piece attacks two things, either a piece or a square (see page 70); also called a **fork**

Draw—no one wins and no one loses. (There are seven ways to draw in tournament chess—one is a **stalemate**, which we learn about in this book.)

En passant—a special capture only pawns can make (see page 56)

Endgame—many of the pieces have come off the board; the end of the game

File—vertical row of squares

Fork—see **double attack**

Hanging pieces—pieces that can be captured for free, or pieces that mean you will win material by capturing them

Helper mate—a checkmate using two pieces: one piece gives check while the other guards that piece

Home square—the place on the board where that piece is first set out

Illegal—not allowed; against the rules

Kingside—the half of the board from the king to the edge (e-file to h-file)

Long-range pieces—the rook, bishop, and queen, which can all move as far as they like each turn

Mate—common, shortened way of saying "checkmate"

Material—another word for pieces or points

Middle game—usually arises after at least one side has castled and both sides have **developed** minor pieces

Notation—a way to write your moves down in chess language (see page 60)

Opening—the beginning stage of the game

Opposition—an odd number of squares in between two kings (see page 36)

Outflank—go around with your king (see page 37)

Pawn promotion—a pawn gets to the other side and turns into a queen, rook, bishop, or knight; it cannot stay a pawn or become a king (see page 16)

Pin—three pieces are in a line and the middle piece cannot move because it would leave the back piece open to attack (see page 80)

Queenside—the half of the board from the queen to the edge (d-file to a-file)

Rank—horizontal row of squares

Relative pin—a pin where the back piece is not the king (so the middle piece could move, but the back piece would be likely to get captured)

Skewer—three pieces in a row, but the piece in the middle is the more valuable piece (see page 80)

Stalemate—the king is NOT in danger, but he cannot move anywhere safely. No other piece of the same color as that king can move. It is the side's turn who cannot move. Instead of passing, the game ends in a draw.

Strategy—a plan to make your pieces work together

Tactic—a trick or a combination of tricks to help you quickly win material or the game

Trade—an exchange of pieces of equal value; for example, you capture a queen and then you immediately lose your queen

Chapter 1
Piece Movement

Pawn Football

Pawns are little guys, but they have special powers: if one reaches the other side of the board, it can become a new piece. We call this **pawn promotion** (see below). The purpose of this game is to practice moving and capturing pawns. The goal is to win by getting one of your pawns to the other side first! You can also win by capturing all your opponent's pawns.

About this activity

When a pawn is promoted (that is, when it gets to the other side of the board), you can replace it with a queen, rook, bishop, or knight. It cannot stay a pawn or become a king. Most people choose to make their pawn a queen because she is the most powerful piece!

This game is for two players.

Fun fact

Theoretically, you can get nine queens on your side in a game of chess! If all eight pawns reach the other side, they can become queens, and if your original queen doesn't get captured, you'll have nine queens in total.

1 In this game, you will start out with four white pawns against four black pawns. Place the white ones on c2, d2, e2, and f2, and the black ones on c7, d7, e7, and f7. White always goes first. Take turns with your partner—remember that pawns can only move one square at a time, unless it's their first move, when they can go forward two squares, if you want (see page 9).

2 Any of your pawns can try to reach the other side. They may have to work together. If one pawn goes it alone, he will definitely get captured by the opposing team…

One way to keep them safe is to create a pawn chain when your pawns are next to each other on diagonal squares, "holding hands" and protecting each other. As pawns only capture diagonally forward, they also protect diagonally forward. If one of your pawns is captured, the neighboring pawn will just capture the opponent's pawn right back. The pawn at the bottom that is not protected is called the base.

Here, if the black pawn on e5 captures the white pawn on f4, then the white pawn on e3 will capture Black right back! The pawn on d2 is the base.

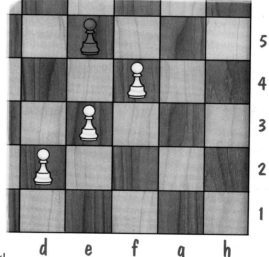

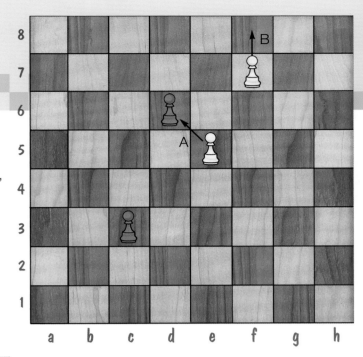

3 In this position, for example, let's say you have White. You could capture a pawn (move A), or you could try to run to the other side and promote your pawn (move B). What would you do? Run! It's better to create a new queen than to capture a single pawn—especially since she'll probably be able to capture the pawn herself!

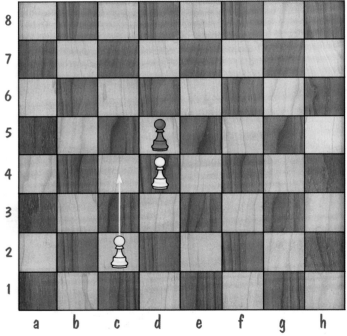

4 Remember, pawns that are head to head are frozen, meaning they cannot move. But since they capture diagonally one square away, even a frozen pawn can capture! In this diagram, don't push your pawn on c2 two steps—it'll just be taken by the pawn on d5!

Variations

Once you've mastered this four-pawn football game, try it with five, then six, seven, and, finally, eight pawns. (Pawns must always face each other—no pawn should start facing an empty square.) Later, you could even include the kings (start them on their home squares, e1 and e8) and see if you can win, like in a real chess match!

5 A problem you could run into is if all your pawns get frozen. You could just call that a draw! Bow to your partner and say, "Good game." Then, switch colors and play again!

Face-Off

Sometimes people confuse the rook and the bishop. They each have their own abilities, and this game will help you learn the different ways that they move around the chessboard. The goal of this game is to capture everything! The first person who captures all of their opponent's pieces wins.

About this activity

The two pieces themselves are very different—the rook is short and round, while the bishop is tall and pointy.

Rooks can move up and down the board and from side to side, so they are worth a little more than bishops (see pages 10 and 11), which can only move diagonally, staying on the color they started on. Both pieces are allowed to go as far as they want, and they can both go backward, but they can't jump over other pieces.

You can play this game with two players—or why not have two teams of two players taking turns?

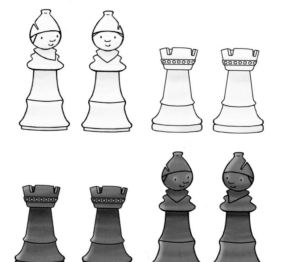

1 For this game, you will only need two rooks and two bishops of each color.

2 Set up the white rooks on e1 and e2, and the white bishops on e3 and e4. Then put the black rooks on e8 and e7 and the black bishops on e6 and e5. Everyone is facing each other on the e-file!

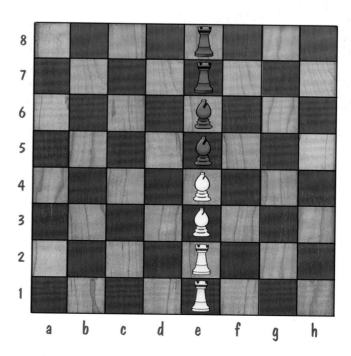

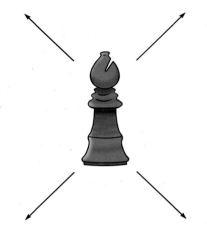

3

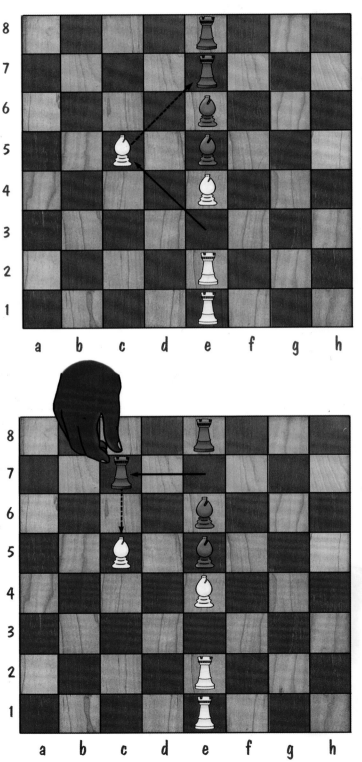

On the first move of this game, no one can make a capture. White gets to go first, and in chess, that usually means White is the first to attack! Here is an example game with just a few moves. Bishops move and attack diagonally, so the bishop that has moved to c5 is now aiming at the black rook on e7, shown by the dotted-line arrow.

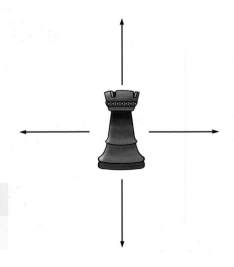

4

To protect his rook, Black moves it to c7 and attacks the bishop! See how the rook is now aiming at c5?

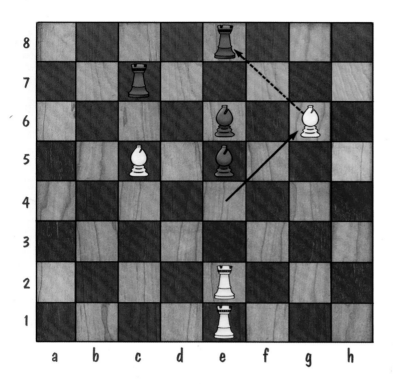

White could save the bishop by moving it off the rook's file and out of the rook's aim—but she could also move her other bishop to the square g6 so that it aims at the rook on e8!

When you're playing, notice that once the bishops move out of the way, the rooks will be lined up with each other on the e-file. If there is only one bishop in between those rooks, be careful moving it!

Variation

This game can be played by removing one of the rooks from each side and replacing it with a queen instead. The queen is the most powerful piece on the board! Generally, the side that loses its queen loses the game. (Of course this is not always true so, above all, NEVER give up!)

Fun fact

Along with the queen, the rook and the bishop are called long-range pieces, because they are the only ones that may travel long distances in a single move.

Rookie Cookie

The rook can go as far as it wants, forward, backward, or sideways, so it's good at attacking your opponent's pieces from a distance! In this activity the Rookie Cookie is very hungry and it wants to capture and eat all the black pieces on the board. And they can't run away! They are placed on the board like statues just waiting to be eaten!

About this activity

Play this game by yourself and see how quickly you can "eat up" the other pieces just by moving forward, backward, and sideways.

Rooks are like speedy cars: they like straight roads to go really fast. But because they can't get out at the beginning of the game, they need to wait until some pawns have been captured so they can move easily across the board.

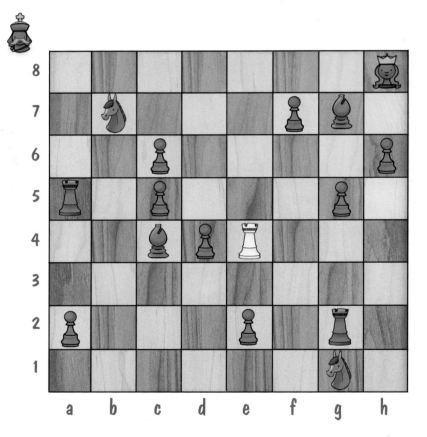

1 Use a rook of one color, let's say white, and all the opposing color's pieces, minus the king. You can place the pieces randomly on the chessboard, as long as everyone occupies a different square. Because the king can never be captured, he'll sit on the sidelines during this game.

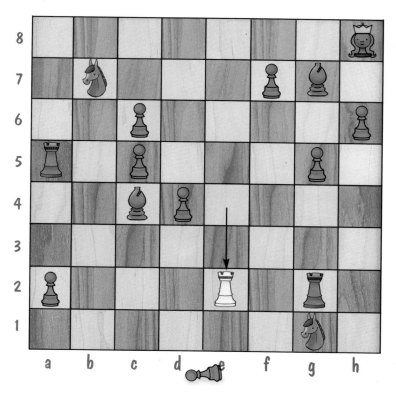

The Rookie Cookie is very hungry, and wants to eat a piece (cookie) every move. He can only eat one piece at a time though. Remember, rooks can go forward, backward, or side to side as far as they want to go, without jumping. So let's have your rook on e4 go down and capture that pawn on e2!

Even though the black knight, bishop, and rook are aiming at the white rook, they cannot capture it in this game, because the Rookie Cookie has frozen all the cookies. Which piece should he eat next? Sometimes there will be a choice.

3 If you get to a point where the Rookie Cookie cannot eat another piece, you should make a plan. This means you will line up with a piece to eat on his next turn. This is what real chess players do all the time!

Variations

There are a lot of variations. You can play the Cookie game with a rook, bishop, queen, or knight! If you are playing with a friend, you could see who eats all the pieces quickest. Make sure you set up the pieces randomly, and take turns being the Rookie Cookie!

Knight Races

Knights are funny. They can jump over pieces, but they can't reach out and capture the piece that's directly in front of them! In this game you are practicing the knight's L-shaped move while trying to travel across the board to the home square of your opponent's knight. Whoever gets there first wins! You also win if you capture the other player's knight on the way.

About this activity

Knights are known for the special way they move. To practice, play this racing game. You can count out "one, two, turn" to plan your path.

Remember that knights only capture what they land on top of, not what they have jumped over! Knights will always change square color when they move.

Play this game with a partner.

Start with one white knight on b1, and one black knight on b8. That's all you need! The knight on b1 must reach b8 to win, and the knight on b8 must reach b1.

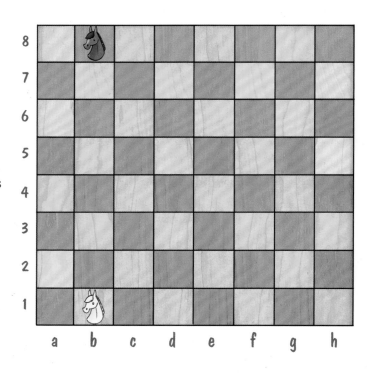

Both knights might start out by simply moving "one, two, turn" toward the other side of the board. They can continue along this way, even bumping into each other as neighbors, "Hello, dear!" "Hello, nice day!" while never bothering each other. Be careful you don't land somewhere the other knight can capture you—that would be an unfortunate surprise!

3 Soon, the knights will near the other side. Once they do, a big plan must be made. The knights are not allowed to jump off the board. And just landing on the first or eighth rank does not win the game. In order to get onto your partner's home square, you have to take a few moves dancing around to prepare. Take a look at this position. How should White proceed? Well, he'll have to do this funny move and step backward to c6 before he can go forward to the home square.

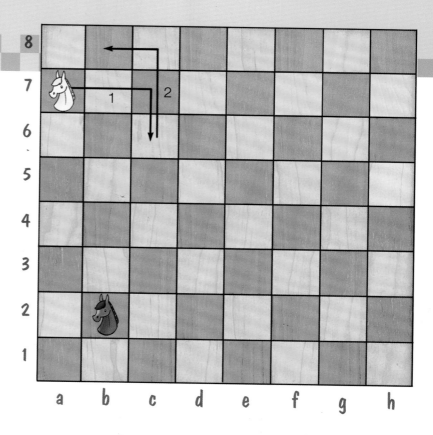

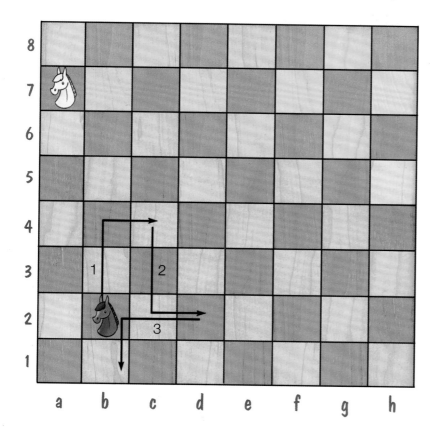

4 Black is in a similar predicament. Although he is right next to the square he wants to reach, he needs to make three moves to achieve his goal. There are many ways to reach b1, but even the quickest paths will take three turns. Here is one example. Follow the arrows to see where he goes.

5 Remember that knights can move in any direction, so long as they go in a capital L-shape: one, two, turn. Usually your index finger and thumb are the right length if you want to measure it out with your hand!

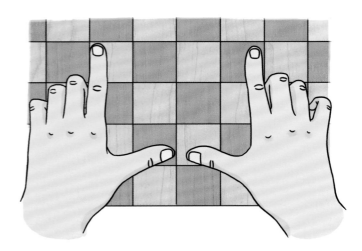

6 Practice the L-shaped move some more by turning your hands over and checking out all the different ways your knight could move: backward, forward, upside down, inside out, right-side in… So you can try going sideways sometimes, not just straight forward.

Variations

An easier variation is to play where one knight must only reach the other side of the board rather than the home square. A more challenging variation would be to play with both knights. Start one white knight on b1 and the other on g1, and the black knights on b8 and g8. Both knights have to get to the opponent's home squares first to win.

Capturing Game

This is a great game for newer chess players. You get to practice capturing—and your math, too! In this activity, play chess as normal, but count up the pieces' point values as you capture them. Whoever first gets 20 points or more wins.

About this activity

Generally in chess, the player who can capture the most pieces will find it easier to trap the king and win. Sometimes trapping the king can take a long time, but as this activity is all about capturing as many pieces as possible, it will go quickly!

In a regular chess game, you usually want to capture any piece that isn't being guarded by another—that is, one that will capture your piece right back. This game helps you to identify the most valuable captures possible.

You should play this game with a partner—although you could also play against yourself to practice your math.

1 In chess, each piece has a point value as you can see in the artwork above. The king is the most valuable, but doesn't have a number, because you can't capture him! Instead, if you **checkmate** (see page 13) and trap him, then you win the whole game!

9 + 1 + 3 + 3 + 3 + 1 = 20

2 Remember, any combination of captured pieces that adds up to 20 or more points wins. For example, you could capture a queen, a pawn, a bishop, two knights, and another pawn, which equals 20 points.

Variations

Speed up your game by making the winner the first person to capture ten, or even six points.

If you are playing someone who is much better than you, give them a "handicap." This just means they would need to capture more points than you. For example, decide that you could win the game if you capture ten points, but they would have to capture 15.

You can also time the game, and whoever has the most points when time is up wins.

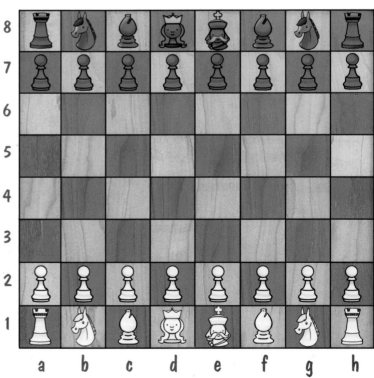

3

Set up the pieces in their normal starting positions.

4 Let's say you are White and start by playing pawn to e4. Then Black plays pawn to e5. No captures yet, but begin looking for pieces to capture. Think about what will happen when you start capturing. If you strike first, will you get captured? Are you closer to 20 points than your opponent? If you are, then sacrificing a small piece might be worthwhile. If pieces of equal value are exchanged, this is called a **trade**.

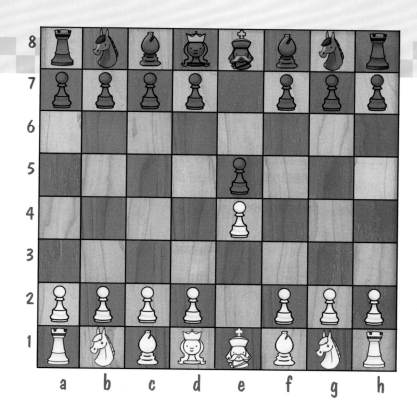

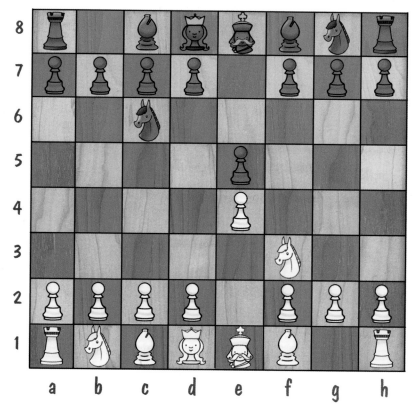

5 You now play knight to f3. You are already threatening to capture someone—do you see which one? That's right—the pawn on e5! Black plays knight out to c6. Should you take the black pawn on e5 now? No! If you do, the black knight will take your knight right back, and you will lose three points and only gain one, giving your opponent a two-point lead. If the black knight weren't guarding the pawn, you'd definitely take it, and the score would be 1-0!

Eight Queens

The queen is the most powerful piece on the board. She can move in eight different directions, as far as she wants, so she is very good at attacking a lot of squares around her. In this game you are trying to set up eight queens on the board in such a way that none of them can attack another. It's a tricky task so you might want to ask a friend to help you.

About this activity

This is a pattern-recognition type of game. It is only about setting up the pieces on the board in the right positions—you do not move or play a game with them.

Because the queen can move in every direction and as many squares as she likes, you will see how tricky it is to put eight queens on the board in squares where they are safe from one another.

Remember how powerful queens are—the only thing they cannot do is jump like the knight!

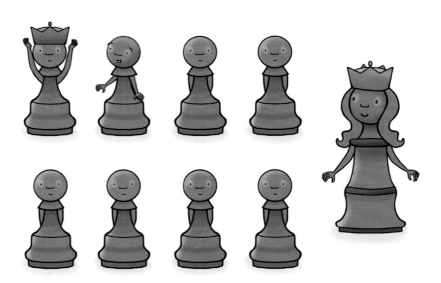

1 Use a regular chessboard. Now take out eight pawns of one color and pretend they are queens. You do not need any other pieces. You can play this activity by yourself, in a pair, or with a whole group, so long as you cooperate and help each other discover the solution. There are many solutions actually. And once you find one, you may find the others more quickly.

2 Think about how queens move—they can go in any direction and as far as they like—but remember, they don't move like knights. So try setting up your "queens" in knight positions from each other, and you will be well on your way to solving this puzzle!

3 Unfortunately, it's not so simple. You'll have to double-check yourself to see if any of the "queens" could "capture" another. If so, start over. Maybe place the first queen on a1 and go around the board plopping pawns down in knights' moves away. Soon, you'll notice a problem: not every queen can be a knight's move from the next. (If they are, some of the queens would be able to capture others!)

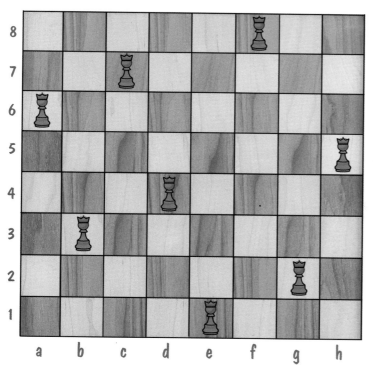

 Variation

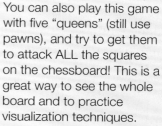

You can also play this game with five "queens" (still use pawns), and try to get them to attack ALL the squares on the chessboard! This is a great way to see the whole board and to practice visualization techniques.

4 This diagram shows one solution, with no queen able to capture any other. There are alternative solutions but you'll have to find them out for yourself! Do you see how many queens are a knight's move away from each other and how many aren't?

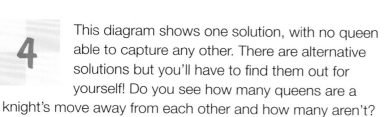

Pieces, No Pawns

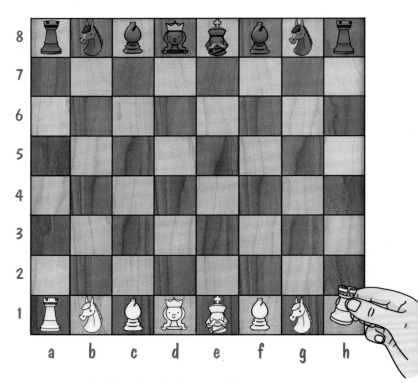

This is like the Capturing Game (see page 27), but without using any pawns! Capturing pieces is a big part of chess. Try to keep your pieces safe while launching them at your opponent, to capture as many of their pieces as possible. This game will also show you how valuable your pawns really are, as you see how difficult it is without them to defend your big pieces from getting captured on the first move of the game!

About this activity

This is a very exciting game, where pieces are getting captured almost every move. The number of points does not matter as much as your ability to look at the whole board and see who might be trying to get you. Remember that you need a double strategy, because you're trying to get them, too.

This is also a capturing game. Whoever captures all the pieces (except for the king—remember, he can never be captured), wins. If you make **checkmate**—that means if you put your opponent's king in danger so that he cannot move, block, or capture in order to escape—that counts, too. (We haven't officially learned about checkmate yet, so don't worry if you can't do it in this activity!)

This is definitely a game for two players.

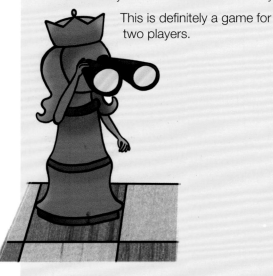

1 Don't forget to bow to your partner before you start, and say, "Good luck!" Set up the pieces as normal, but do not put any pawns on the board.

2 Let's look at an example, with you playing as White. On move one, White can make three captures. Either rook could take a black rook, or you could play queen takes queen!

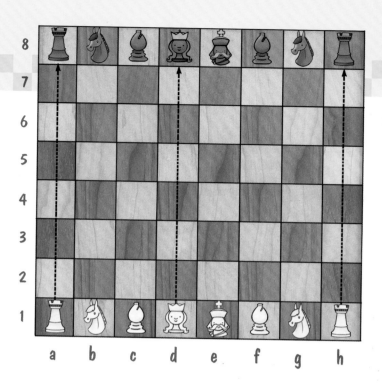

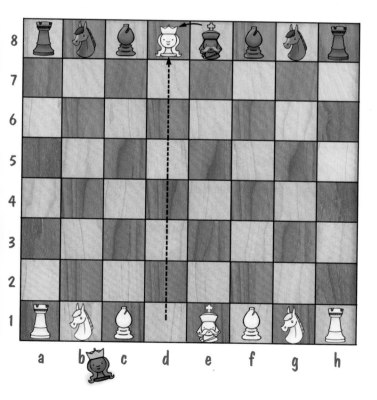

3 What would happen if your queen took the black queen? It's **check**—the king is in danger—but not **checkmate**, because the black king can easily escape from danger. The black king would take your queen right back.

4 Maybe rook takes rook is better! Now, which rook? There might be a whole series of captures here… Having the first move is going to be an advantage if Black just copies what White does. Once the king is in check, though, you must move, block, or capture to escape from danger. You can't copy your opponent if you're busy getting out of check!

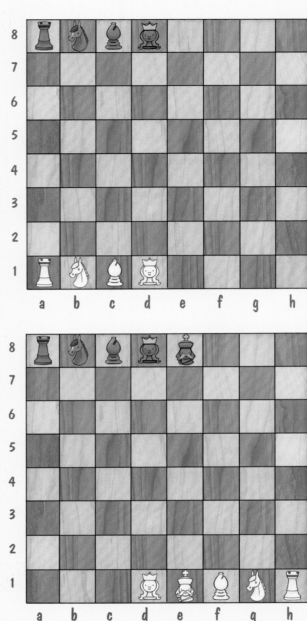

Variations

You could play on only half the board without the king. Simply start on one half, say a1–d1 and place down your rook, knight, bishop, and queen. Still no pawns. Your opponent would have his/her pieces facing yours. Pieces could still travel over the whole board. You win by capturing everything.

Another possibility is to play with only one of each piece, still no pawns, and have the rooks, knights, and bishops not face each other.

Opposing Kings

In this game, both players try to reach their opponent's home rank. That sounds simple—but kings can never touch and must remain one or more squares apart from each other. If one king gets too close to the other, he enters the other king's "forcefield," which is not allowed!

About this activity

Because a king moves one step at a time (see page 12), he attacks all the squares around him. You may never put your own king in danger—it is **illegal** (against the rules of chess) to capture a king. Therefore, the two kings can never touch!

This means that once your king is facing your opponent's king, one square away, the other king will not be able to move toward you—if it's his turn, he can only move sideways or back.

As White goes first, she should always be able to find a way to win, so if Black is able to keep White away from the back rank for ten moves, Black wins!

This game can be played by yourself or with a partner.

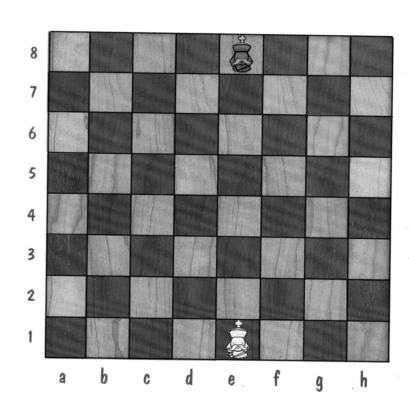

1 Use only one king of each color on your chessboard. The kings start out with White on e1 and Black on e8.

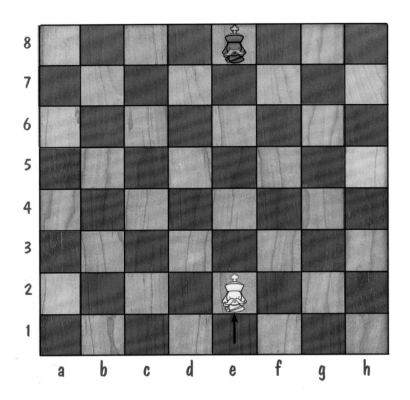

2

First, White must play king to e2. This move makes an odd number of squares between the kings and, if you continue to play correctly, it should allow you to win. No other moves work! This idea is called **opposition**—we say that White has now taken opposition on Black.

3

As the kings get closer, White will continue to make opposition on Black until they come face to face (with one square between them).

Now it will be Black's turn to move. He will have to move to one side or go backward, because if he were to move forward (onto one of the squares marked with a star), he would put himself in danger (see page 35)—which is an **illegal** move!

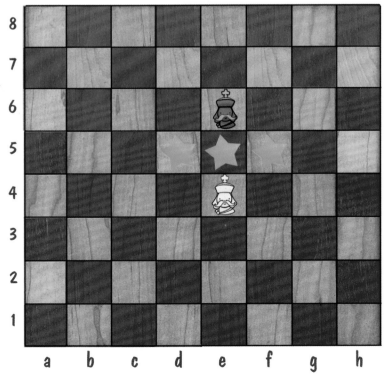

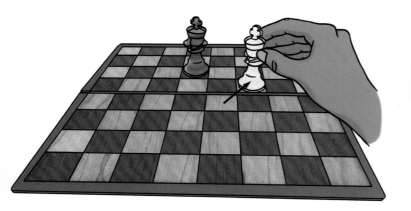

4 Once Black moves to the side, White can move forward on the other side. Moving around in this way is called **outflanking**. So White outflanks Black by going diagonally forward and gets a rank closer to the end! If Black moves to d6, then White should go to f5!

5 Go back to the start, playing as White. What happens if you play king to f2 instead? Black will take opposition on you, by moving the black king to f8, and this will be super-annoying, because he will shut you out! As you get closer to each other, Black can maintain the opposition, and never let you in. Play through the moves to see why.

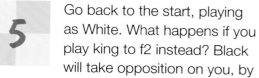

Variations

Start the kings on any square along the first rank. Make the game even harder by choosing specific squares for the white king to land on. This is a challenging activity. Try it a few times; always be sure you are counting the squares in between the kings to see if you can make opposition on your opponent!

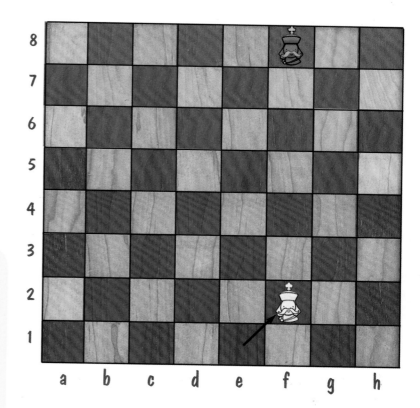

Chapter 2
Tricky Rules & Cool Vocab

Three Checks Wins ☺☺☺

This game is all about threatening your opponent's king, which is called putting him in **check**. You win by being the first to put your opponent's king in danger three times. This means you're focusing on attack and do not need to worry too much about losing pieces in this game.

About this activity

By putting your opponent's king in **check**—that is, putting him in danger—you force your opponent to escape from danger rather than attack you. Check is a very powerful move!

Remember, you are never allowed to capture the king, so if he's in danger, you need to announce it by calling out "CHECK!". Your opponent then has to capture, block, or move to escape.

If your opponent makes a move that keeps the king in check, that is **illegal** (against the rules). Let them take it back and try to find a safe move.

You will be doing some really great chess planning! In chess you will often think, "If I go here, then what would he/she do?"

This game is for two players.

CHECK!

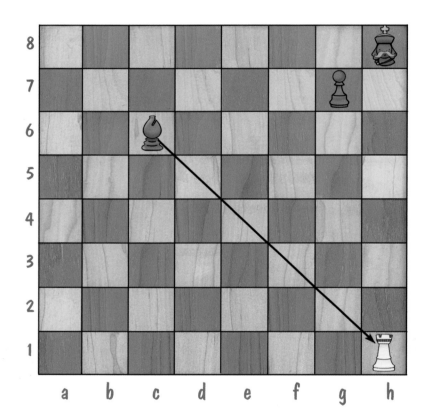

1 In a moment, you will set up the chessboard with all the pieces in their home positions, but, before you start, think about the three ways that the king can escape from the danger when he is in check.

First, he can try to CAPTURE the piece that is attacking him. Here, the white rook has the king in check, but the black bishop can capture the rook.

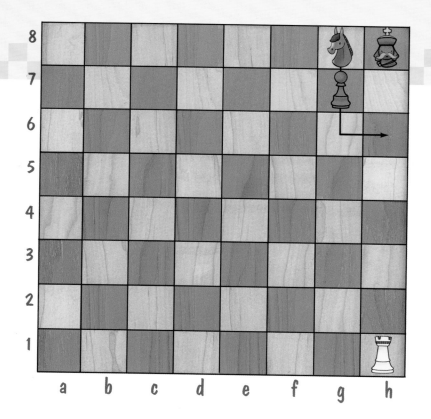

His second option is to BLOCK the danger by moving another of his pieces in the way of the attacker. So here the black knight must move to h6 to block the rook.

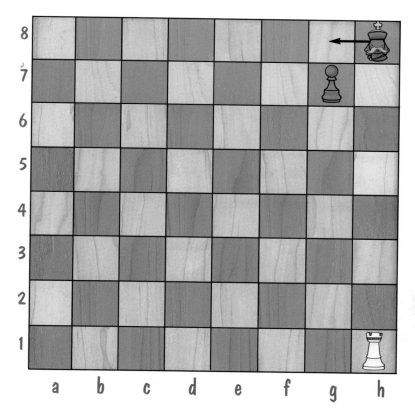

Finally, he can MOVE—that is, run away to a safer position. Remember, he can only move one square at a time! In this case, the king must move to g8.

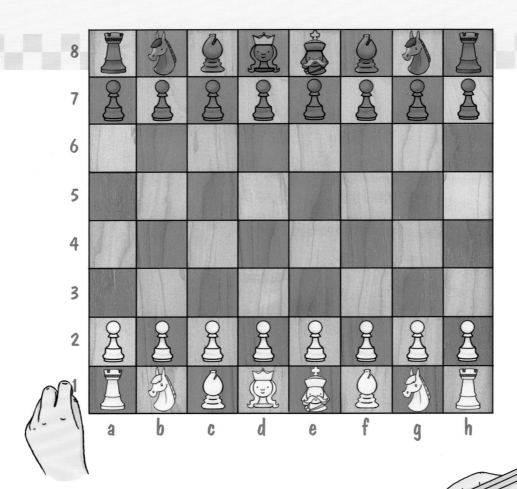

2

Now set up your board with all the pieces in their home positions. If you like, you can get a paper and pencil to tally your checks.

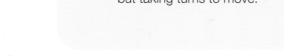

Variations

You can also play five checks wins, to make the game a little longer. Or try team chess, with two players on each team, sitting at the same board together, but taking turns to move.

3 This game favors the person who can **develop** their pieces (move their pieces from their starting positions) the quickest. If you can aim at the king straight away, it may be a good idea to sacrifice a piece just to make check! If White moves his bishop to c4, he will be aiming at f7.

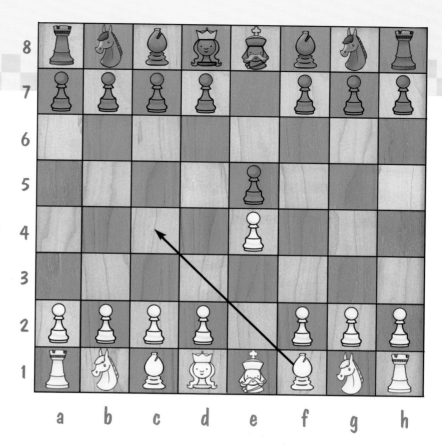

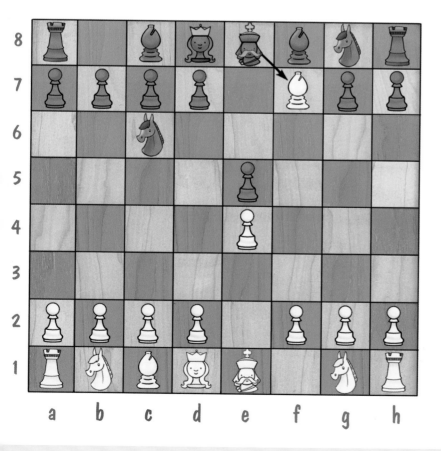

4 Once the bishop captures the pawn on f7, White will say, "Check!" and earn a tally mark on the score sheet. Black can capture the bishop with the king to get himself out of danger, but in this game it's worth White losing that bishop, since it draws the king out from his starting position. What can White do next to get the king in check again? (The answer is at the bottom of the page.)

Solution to (4):
When the king moves to f7, the white queen can move to f3 or h5 to put him in check again.

Create-a-Mate

How do you win a game of chess? **Checkmate!** Practice this vital skill in the following activity. Place two pieces anywhere so that they create a checkmate on the opposing king. There are lots of ways to do this!

About this activity

- - - - - - - - - - - - - - -

The most common way of making checkmate is called helper mate: one piece attacks the king, and another piece helps out by preventing the king from escaping! Here you will see how certain pieces can work well together, both to attack and defend.

You can play all by yourself, or with a partner or group of four, as long as you can cooperate!

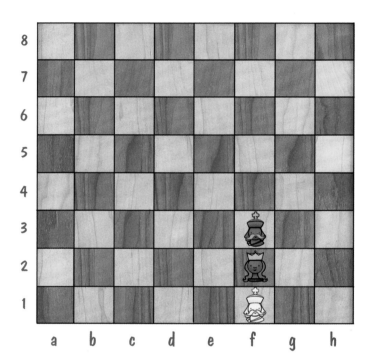

1 The first checkmate we're going to practice involves the black queen and king, and the white king. The black queen gives **check**—this means that she is putting the white king in danger. Remember, there are three ways to escape from check: move, block, or capture (see pages 40–1)! But the king cannot MOVE—wherever he goes, he will still be in danger from the queen. He cannot BLOCK: there are no squares in between the king and queen. And he cannot CAPTURE in this position, because the black king is protecting the queen—remember that the two kings cannot touch, because it's against the rules (see page 35)!

The king cannot escape from check—this means that it's checkmate. We call this position the Queen Sandwich checkmate, because it's like the kings are the bread and the queen is the filling.

2 You can use the same trick if the king is in the corner, only this time you must line up your king and queen diagonally. Again, he is in mate (that's short for checkmate), because there is no escape.

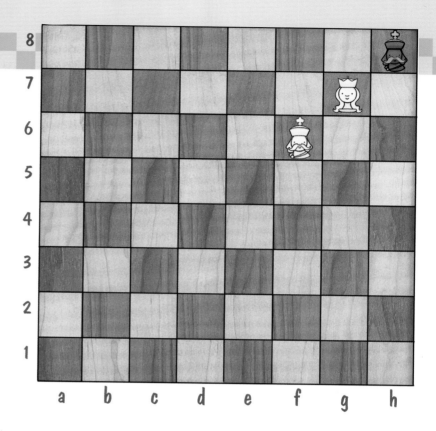

3 An alternative to the Queen Sandwich is when the attacking pieces are not directly in line with the king. It's a messy sandwich (like a Sloppy Joe!), but still mate! As long as someone is protecting the queen, it will be checkmate. You can use any piece to protect her. These types of checkmates are called helper mates. That's because one piece puts the king in check, and the other piece helps by protecting!

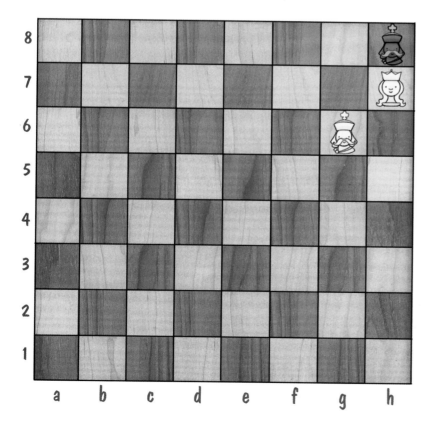

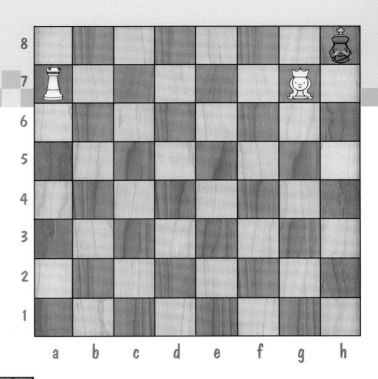

4 Now you try it! On your board, place a black king on h8. This king is not allowed to play and travel around the board. It is your job to put a queen and a rook on the board anywhere you like, so that they are creating checkmate. Start by putting one piece down to aim at the king and say check. Which piece is more powerful? The next one you place can protect the first! There are many answers. If you have something like the diagram here, you rock!

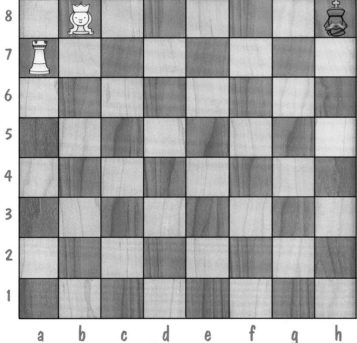

6 Now try some other checkmates. Instead of using a queen and a helper, try using other combinations—for example, four pawns; two bishops and a king; and a rook and a knight only.

5 Another type of checkmate is the "back rank mate." Using the same pieces, you could create a checkmate without even touching the king. As long as the king is in danger and cannot move, block, or capture, it's checkmate. He's trapped on the very last row of the board, so that's why we say "back rank mate."

Variations

Practice other mates on your own. Try checkmating the king on g8 instead of h8. Try making checkmate with a rook, bishop, and king of one color, and a pawn and king of the opposite color. Count how many different possible checkmate positions there are for each variation. You'll find lots!

Loyds

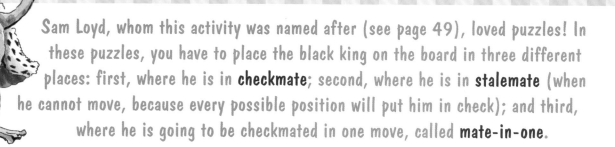

Sam Loyd, whom this activity was named after (see page 49), loved puzzles! In these puzzles, you have to place the black king on the board in three different places: first, where he is in **checkmate**; second, where he is in **stalemate** (when he cannot move, because every possible position will put him in check); and third, where he is going to be checkmated in one move, called **mate-in-one**.

About this activity

If you're not able to win, it's better to try to draw than lose. When you've only got a few pieces left, you might be able to get into a position from which you cannot move without putting yourself into check (which isn't allowed). When you can't move any of your pieces, you haven't lost—you've made a special type of draw called a **stalemate**.

Remember that in a real game, you don't want to make a stalemate if you're winning!

As well as practicing stalemates and checkmates, you also need to learn to think one move ahead. Sometimes the king appears safe at first, but after one move by his opponent, he'll be in checkmate. This is called **mate-in-one**.

You can play this game by yourself or with a friend.

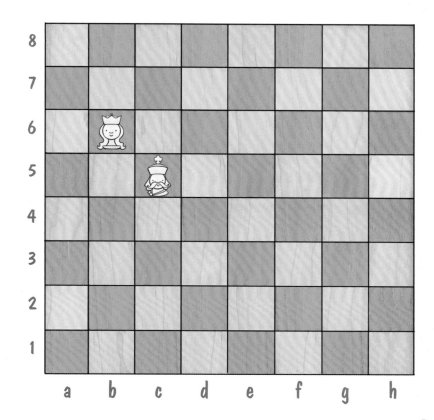

1 With the white queen on b6 and the white king on c5, there is one position in which the black king is in checkmate—wherever he moves he will put himself in danger, which he cannot do. See what happens when you place him on a6: he's in check and has no escape so White wins the game.

2 Placing him somewhere where he's in stalemate is slightly trickier. He must not be in check, but it must be a square from which every move will put him in check. That square is a8: wherever he moves he would be putting himself in check by the queen, so he has no legal moves. Stalemates often happen when the king is in the corner because he has the fewest number of escape squares there.

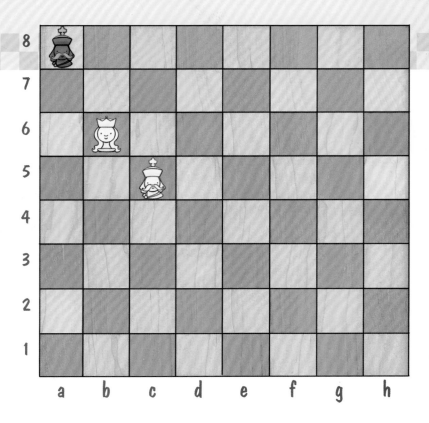

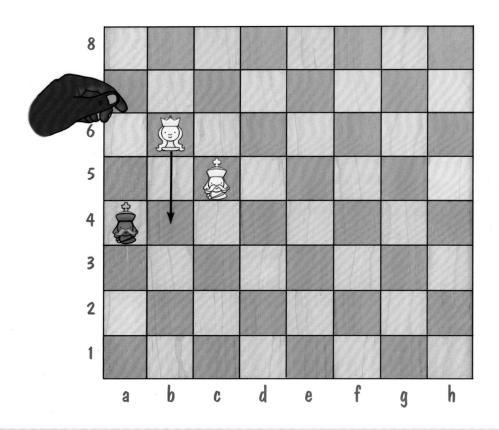

3 Even harder is seeing the position in which he will be in checkmate after one move by White (mate-in-one). See what happens if you place the black king on a4 and White moves the queen to b4: he's in check. Because he cannot escape, it is also checkmate.

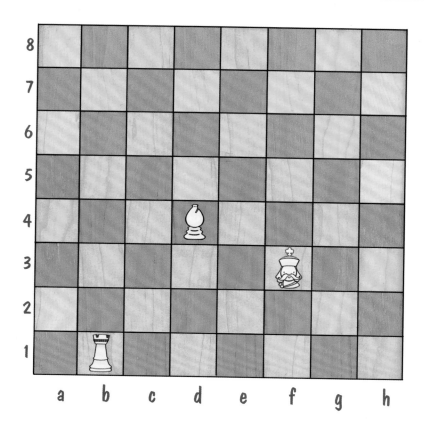

4 Now you try without any help! Place the white king on f3, the white bishop on d4, and the white rook on b1. Where would you place the black king for checkmate, stalemate, and mate-in-one? (The answers are at the bottom of the page.)

5 You can make your own Loyd puzzle! Start with a checkmate, then work backward! Use as many pieces as you need. When you're ready, pluck the king off the board and hand it to a friend. Say, "Here you go, friend! Where should you place him [the king] so he's in mate and stalemate?" I bet you could even stump your parents!

Solution to (4):
For checkmate, place the king on f1; for stalemate, place the king on a8; and for mate-in-one, place the king on h3 and move the rook to h1.

Castling Game

Castling is a trick you can do only once during your game. It's a way of getting your king safe so he hides behind a wall of pawns while everyone else does the attacking. In the castling game, your job is to castle first—whoever does, wins! Read the rules below carefully before playing to learn how to use this special move.

About this activity

Castling is the only time in chess when the king gets to go two steps, and the only time you can move two pieces in the same move, as the rook jumps over him at the same time! The king ends up safe while being protected by the rook beside him and the knight out front, always on the look out.

This game is for two players.

Castling rules

There are a lot of rules surrounding this amazing move:

- You can only castle once.

- You can't castle if your king or rook (the rook you want to castle with) has ever taken a move.

- You can't castle if there are pieces in between your king and rook.

- You can't castle if your king is in check.

- You can't castle if the square that your king would pass through when castling would put him in check.

- You can't castle if your king lands on a square that puts him in check. (That should make sense—you are never allowed to put your king in danger in chess!)

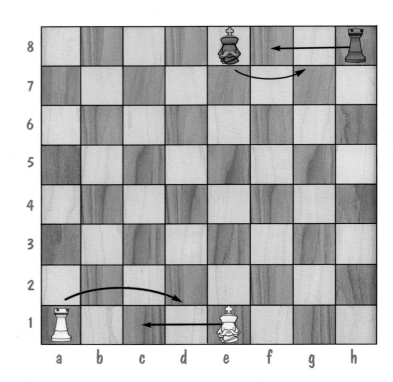

1 So how do you castle? First, your king and rook must start from their home squares. Then the king moves two toward the rook, and the rook jumps over and lands right next to the king.

Remember, you can only do this move according to the castling rules—see the box on the left.

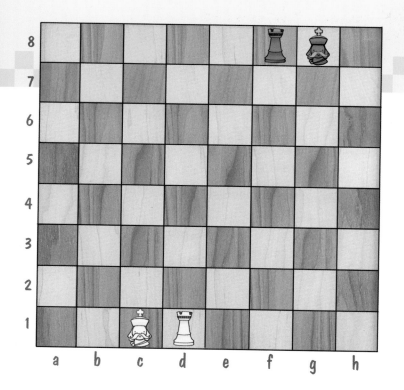

2
For both Black and White, there are two directions in which you could castle. Here, White has castled queenside (toward the queen's home square), also called castling "long." Black has castled kingside (away from the queen), or castled "short." (White can also castle kingside, and Black could castle queenside, using their other rooks, not shown here.)

3
There are two strategies to use in the castling game. First, you can develop your pieces as soon as possible—that is, try to move the pieces that are between your king and your rook—then castle (and win!). The second option is to prevent your opponent from castling by making a check where the king would have to move to escape. Remember, once the king has been moved, he can never castle.

4
Now let's look at an example of the castling game! Follow the numbered arrows to see how the game progresses. (You might want to follow the moves using your own chess set, too.) Black has focused on her plan to move the pieces between her king and rook quickly out of the way so that she can castle. Note that Black is planning to castle short (kingside). White is not sure about her plan, so it looks like Black will win.

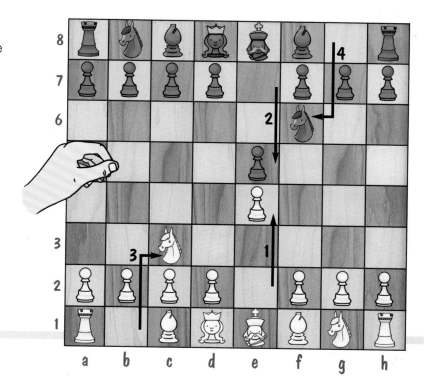

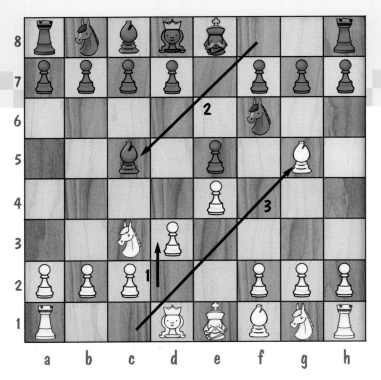

5 Now if White were clever, she would develop her pieces between the king and kingside rook. However, she has moved the wrong knight first (in step 4 on the previous page). White next plays her pawn to d3. She is planning to castle queenside! This is fine, but it's not the quickest way to castle. Black plays the bishop to c5. After White puts her bishop out to g5, what should Black do to win?

6 Black castles—so he wins the game! Here, Black has castled kingside. See how the king has moved two squares to land on g8, and the rook has jumped over him and landed right next door?

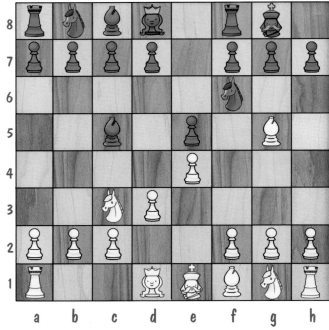

Top tip

Professional chessplayers almost always castle! They like to keep a row of pawns in front of the king and rook as a blanket for the king to snuggle. He's safe and warm in his castle.

7 In regular chess games (that is, not the Castling Game), castling is really smart for your king most of the time, but just occasionally it's actually a bad idea. Can you think when that might be? Well, don't castle if your opponent is ready to checkmate you after you do so!

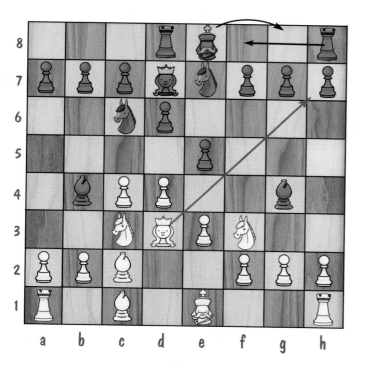
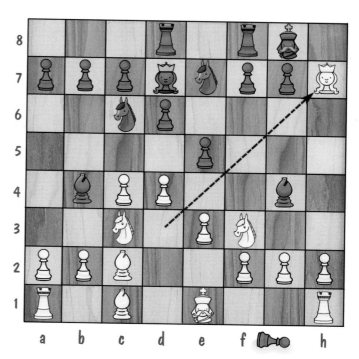

8 Here's an example of this (in a regular chess game). Black castles — but the white queen is aiming at the pawn on h7. So on the next move, the queen captures the pawn (see second diagram): now the king is in check… and it's also checkmate! He cannot move or block to escape; he cannot even capture the queen, because if he did, he'd put himself into check again (the white bishop on c2 is aiming at h7 as well), which is not allowed. White wins — Black shouldn't have castled!

9 Now play the castling game for yourself! Play twice: the first time as White, then swap with your partner for the second game and play as Black. If you play properly, you'll discover that White should manage to castle first, because White always starts first. Good luck!

King Travels

In this game, your only job is to keep your king safe as he moves from one corner of the board to the other. Sound easy? Well, he will have to travel, Indiana Jones-style, through a maze of giant hairy spiders and thick cobwebs, ghosts and ghouls and mummies (that is, er, queens...)! The king is an old man, and though he is the most important, he is not the most powerful piece on the board, as he can only go one step at a time!

About this activity

The goal is to move the white king from a1 to h8 without ever putting him in danger—which we now know is called **check**. Remember, putting your own king in check is an **illegal** move—it's not allowed. So if your move puts your king in check, you will have to start the whole maze over!

The king is allowed to capture pieces as he goes along (imagine Indiana fighting his way through!), but he can only move one square at a time (he's a bit older than Indy).

All the other pieces on the board are like statues in this game—they can't move.

You can play by yourself, but it's fun to play in a group and take turns. If the person playing makes an illegal move, they then sit out, and the next person starts from the beginning of the maze. You could make one player the referee, calling out the illegal moves, or you could all do that together.

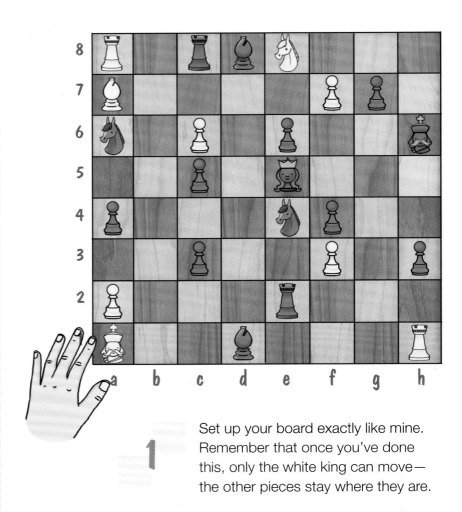

1 Set up your board exactly like mine. Remember that once you've done this, only the white king can move—the other pieces stay where they are.

2 Where might the king go on his first move? He can only travel one square at a time, and he cannot jump over other pieces, so his options are b1 and b2. But one of those moves is illegal—can you see which one?

3 The solution to the puzzle is on page 126, but try to work it out for yourself before looking at it. And remember, if someone makes an illegal move, he/she must take that move back and try a different move. Rewind! You cannot go forward if something illegal happens; you have to go back!

Variations

You can do this yourself: set up five or more black pieces and see if the king can make it safely across. You may need to adjust the position until you have it right. Then, test your friends! Figure out how many moves it would take to get across the board and see if the king can travel safely. You can also play with a timer (or chess clock—see page 63). Whoever can get the king safely across the board the quickest wins.

En Passant Football

Remember how pawns have super powers? Not only can they promote (see page 16), they also have another trick up their sleeve: they can take other pawns in a special move called en passant. Watch very carefully, because this rule is complicated and looks strange! Then have a game of En Passant Football to practice making this move yourself.

About this activity

En passant is when a pawn can capture another pawn next to it. You can use it at any time in the game, but only in a certain situation: if your opponent's pawn has just moved two squares and landed next to your pawn, you can take it! But if they end up next to you after only moving one square forward, than you cannot do en passant.

The En Passant Football game is for two players.

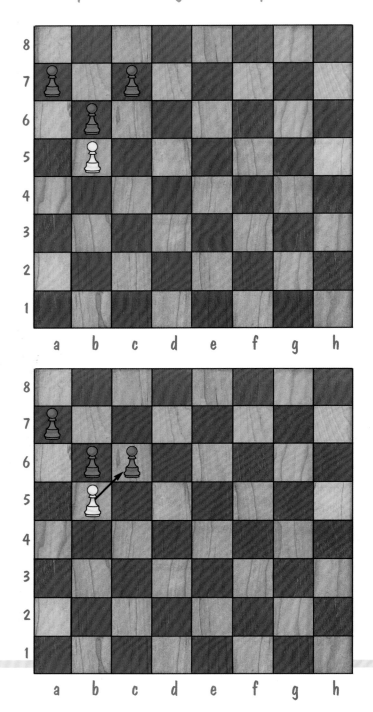

1 Let's look at how en passant works. In the first diagram, White's single pawn is blockading all three of Black's! The middle pawn is frozen (it cannot move forward) and if the a-file or c-file pawn go one space forward here, White can capture it diagonally (as seen in the second diagram).

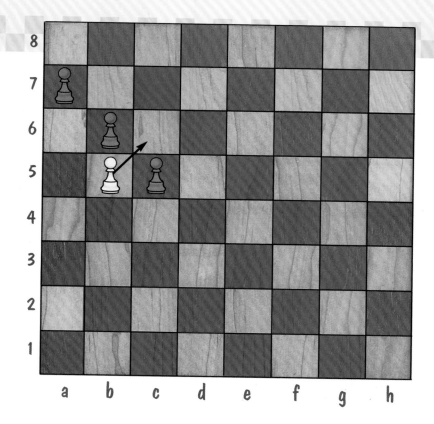

However, if either pawn goes TWO squares forward (for example, in the first diagram here, the pawn on c7 moves to c5), you can still capture it, by moving diagonally, as shown in the second diagram. You don't even touch it! That's en passant.

Can you do en passant?

An easy way to check if you can use en passant is to see if you can answer yes to BOTH of the following questions:

1. Are your pawn and your opponent's pawn side by side?

2. Did your opponent's pawn JUST move two squares from home to get there?

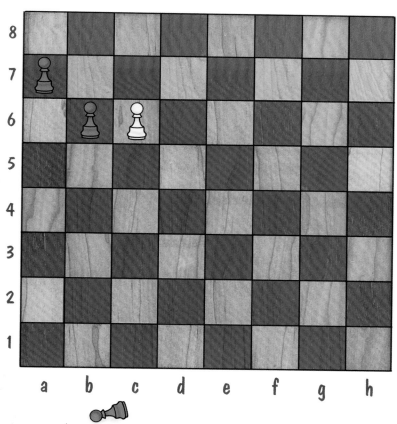

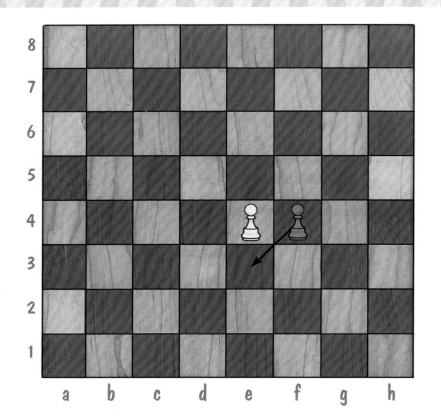

3 Here's another example. White moves from e2 to e4 and lands next to Black on f4. So Black does en passant, capturing the white pawn and moving to e3!

4 Let's look at some different situations. Can White capture en passant in these 4 positions after Black's move (which is shown by an arrow)?

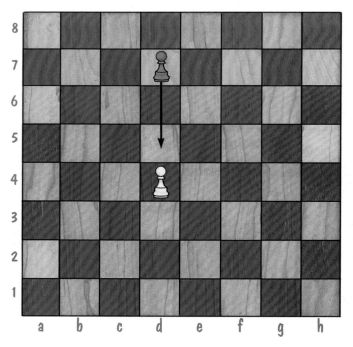

Position 1: NO—Black moves from d7 to d5, and when pawns are head to head, they are frozen and unable to move.

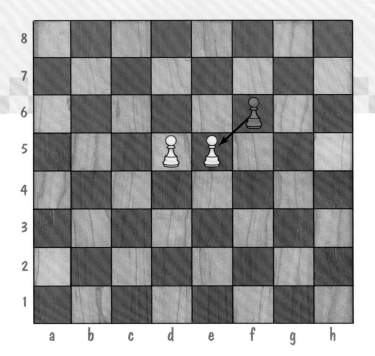

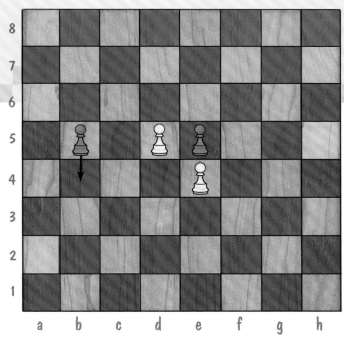

Position 2: NO—the black pawn moves from f6 to e5, capturing the white pawn on e5 from one square away; it is not moving two from home so the pawn on d5 cannot capture it en passant.

Position 3: NO—the black pawn that you are side by side with (on e5) is not moving two squares forward. The b-file pawn is the one moving, from b5 to b4.

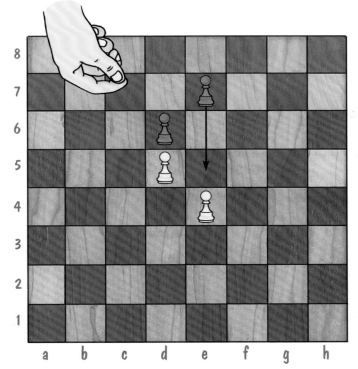

Position 4: YES—now you capture! The black pawn moves two spaces forward from e7 to e5, so you can move your white pawn from d5 to e6, and remove the black pawn from e5 – en passant!

5 Now you're ready to play a game of En Passant Football! It's like Pawn Football (see page 16) but with an extra rule—you will use all eight pawns for both sides, and you can use en passant! Just make sure you can always answer yes to both questions on page 57 before you do it. Set up the pawns on the second and seventh ranks to begin. Whoever gets one pawn to the other side first wins!

Team Chess

Notation is a genius creation that allows you to record your moves. Team Chess is a game where you must use chess notation to describe your moves to your partner. You are not allowed to talk at all! Chess notation is a language you will learn below. The goal is still to checkmate your opponents.

About this activity

This game should be played with four players. You'll need only one chess set and paper and pencils for everyone.

Remember how we listed the "names" of all the squares at the very beginning? That skill will come in handy now, as we learn how to notate.

For your game, you will write down your ideas to your partner. But you can only write down your suggestions as moves, using chess notation. You can't write long sentences in words because your partner would get tired of waiting for you to finish!

1 To record your moves you need to write down the piece that is moving and then the square it lands on. Each piece has a single letter to describe it, usually the first letter of the piece's name. Knights and pawns are different. "Knight" and "king" both start with "k," so we use an N for the knight (the first letter you hear when you say "knight"). And the pawns don't get a capital letter at all! We simply write down the letter and number of the square the pawn moves to.

[blank] = pawn
N = knight
B = bishop
R = rook
Q = queen
K = king

2 To start the game you might move a white pawn two squares forward from e2 to land on e4, so you'd write down **1.e4**.

You write down the white and black moves together in pairs. As White always moves first, there's no need to write down which side makes each move. So if Black now moves a pawn to e5, the first move pair is: **1.e4 e5.**

Then White moves their knight to f3, and Black moves their knight to c6, so for the second pair, you write (on the next line): **2.Nf3 Nc6.**

3 Occasionally in a game, you come across a situation where two pieces of the same kind could move to the same square. In that case, you include their starting file or rank. For example, if two rooks are on the first rank and the one on a1 moved to f1, you would write **Raf1**. If two rooks are on the f-file and the one on f5 moves to f1, you would write **R5f1**.

4 There's some extra notation to add in to show what's happening in the game:

x = capture
+ = check
# = checkmate
0-0 = castles short (see page 50)
0-0-0 = castles long (see page 50)

When pawns capture, just write the file letter where they begin and the square they land on. So a pawn on c4 capturing a knight on d5 would be written as **cxd5**.

5 See if you can work out the notation for the knight's two possible moves. First, note down which piece is moving, so write N (remember, the king is K), then the square he lands on. In this case, it's either f4 or g5 so you notate: **Nf4** or **Ng5**—that's it, simple!

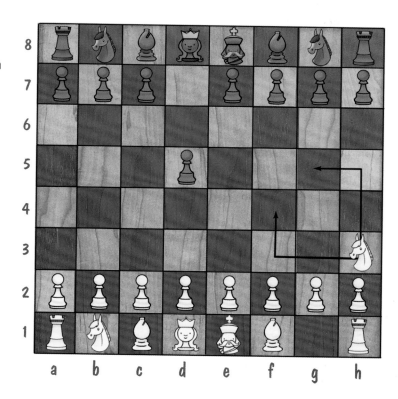

Fun fact

The super-shorthand way to write a pawn capturing a pawn is just to write the file letter and the next file letter. A pawn on c4 capturing a pawn on d5 is written **cd**!

6 Now play a game! Each time, plan your next move with your partner using chess notation only. You might want to set a time limit—maybe a total of five minutes per move.

Tournament Chess

You're ready to play your first proper game of chess: you know all the rules and can write down your moves so it's time to play a tournament with your friends! Now, get serious and see if you can win your first game so no take-backs, no talking, and try your hardest!

About this activity

You will need a chess set, notation paper (or lined paper and draw a vertical line down the middle for white and black moves), and, of course, an opponent.

A chess clock is optional (professionals call it a clock and not a timer, although timing is what it does!) You can get an analog clock (like the one in the artwork) or a digital one.

Top tips

Sit up straight and tall. Before you start your game, try breathing slowly for a minute or so—breathe in through your nose and out your mouth. Tournament chess is very much a sport of mind and body; focusing for a long time is strenuous, and you need to be in good health to do it well!

1 There are some things you must remember when playing tournament chess. Not all of them are rules as such, but to play properly you must follow them.

First of all: no kibitzing. Kibitzing means chatting, so during a chess game there should be no talking about anything, especially your plans. You can't get advice from other people, because that's not fair; plus, you do not want to give away your ideas by telling your opponent what you're up to! Try to keep a "poker" face—don't show in your face that you have spotted a great move or that your opponent has made a mistake.

2 Second is that if you touch a piece, you have to move it, which means you must think before starting your turn. (Although you cannot move your rook, king, bishop, or queen on move one, even if you touch it!) We call this the "touch move rule." If you realize you've moved the wrong piece, it's too late—there's no going back, so always plan before you put your hand near the board. If you touch one of your opponent's pieces, whether with your fingers or your piece, you have to capture it (unless it's against the rules—all the other rules you've learned still apply). If you knock a piece over by mistake and need to fix it, just say, "Adjust," before touching your piece.

3 No giving up! "Tanking" is when you decide you are losing and don't feel like putting in the effort into playing anymore. It is not really fair to you or your opponent. Instead, try to go for a stalemate (see Loyds on page 47) if you can no longer win. Remember that everyone makes mistakes; you could make a huge comeback!

4 Try to notate your game, as one day you might enjoy looking back at it. Notating also helps you analyze the game, and reviewing your chess game with a coach or a friend is probably the quickest way to improve! You can learn tricks and also what mistakes may have been made.

When you notate, write down your opponent's move immediately, then put your pencil down and think about your move. If you think first, you may forget to write down his or her move and it will interrupt your flow.

Variation

Play with the chess clock. A chess clock consists of two clocks linked together so that when one of the clocks is stopped, the other starts. You set your clock for an agreed amount of time—say 30 minutes. Before the game starts, Black chooses the side the clock is placed on and, after shaking hands, Black pushes the button to make White's button stand up (and her clock start ticking).

White takes her turn, and when she's made her move, she presses the button, which stops her clock and starts up Black's clock. When Black finishes, he presses the button, which stops his clock and starts White's. Each turn, your clock starts when your opponent presses down the button. His clock starts when you press yours. Remember to press the clock after you move. Use the same hand that moved the piece to push the button. (No need to slam it!) Remember that if both sides have 30 minutes, your game could last an hour.

When time runs out, the little flag falls (or shows zero on a digital clock). If your time runs out before you can make a checkmate, you lose. If your opponent's time runs out, then your opponent will lose, regardless of the position on the board—unless, of course, someone is making checkmate. Checkmate wins!

Chapter 3
Tactics & Strategy

Take Me! ☺ ☺ ○

YAY!

This game is super fun! It's kind of like opposite chess. In regular chess, you want to capture stuff. If you get more of your opponent's pieces it'll be much easier for you to win, right? But now you want to LOSE your pieces. And if you can lose ALL of your pieces (including the king!), then you WIN! So, opposite chess... Your job is to try to get all your guys captured, and not capture any of your opponent's guys.

About this activity

You'll need to set up the game as you would a regular chess game. All the pieces go on their original squares and move the regular way. If there is a capture on the board, then you must make that capture as your turn!

This game teaches you about **hanging pieces**. These are unguarded or undefended pieces that you can capture without your piece being taken straight back. In regular chess, if you have a choice, you would definitely want to capture a piece where you don't get captured back! That way you begin to dominate the board and you are one step closer to trapping the king.

In this activity you must try to leave your pieces unguarded since, interestingly, that will help you play real chess, because you'll learn to recognize when pieces are hanging (unguarded) and so will remember to protect them. In chess, after learning all the rules, this is the most critical skill to master to become a strong player. It sounds really simple to protect all your pieces but, in fact, it's really hard: hanging pieces are everywhere!

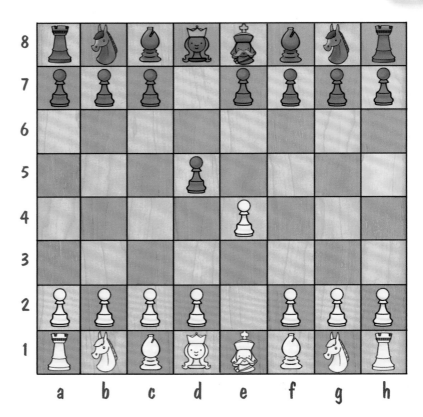

1 Let's look at a few example moves of this game. Afterward, play your own game with a friend! Let's say I'm White and play pawn to e4, and you go pawn to d5. (Chess notation for that would be 1. e4 d5.) You say, "Take me," because my pawn can capture yours! And I HAVE to capture you now. Now it's your turn.

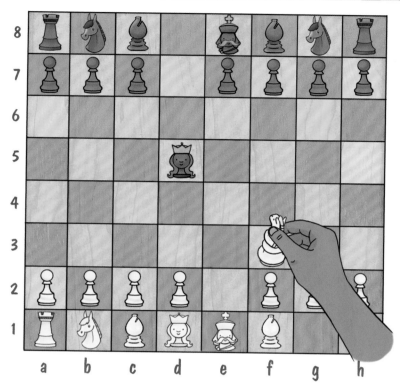

Fun fact

The fancy French term you may hear for a piece that is open to capture is "en prise" (pronounced "on preez").

2 Now, your queen on d8 can capture me, so I say, "Take me!"— and you HAVE to capture me. We still take turns. Even though your queen is out and can capture the entire planet, it is still my turn next. I can't capture anyone, so I just play my knight to f3, and say, "Take me," because your queen on d5 can capture the knight, or the pawn on d2 or even the pawn on a2! You choose which one, but you must capture one of those pieces.

3 Let's say your queen takes the pawn on d2. In normal chess you say, "Check," but here, you say, "Take me!" And now I have to capture your queen. Oh no! I can use my knight, bishop, queen or king… but I have to take it. And you are super-happy: "I lost my queen—awesome! Now she can go on vacation: maybe she'll go snowboarding!"

Ghost Chess

The knight is normally the only piece that can jump over other pieces, but imagine what it would be like if every long-range piece could pass through pieces: it would be as though the pieces had become ghosts that can pass through walls. Play this game and see how much trickier it is if you've got to think about trying to keep yourself safe from all those pieces that are normally hidden away. Try playing Ghost Chess even if it isn't Halloween!

About this activity

Each of your **long-range pieces** (your rooks, queen and bishops) may go through one of your own pieces (but not your opponent's pieces) any time they want to! So, now not only are the knights jumpers, but so are rooks, bishops, and queens!

Checkmate wins the game, just as in a normal game.

Use a complete chess set. You can play this activity by yourself or with a partner.

Top tip

Be flexible and try new things. Sometimes they help you learn in a different way!

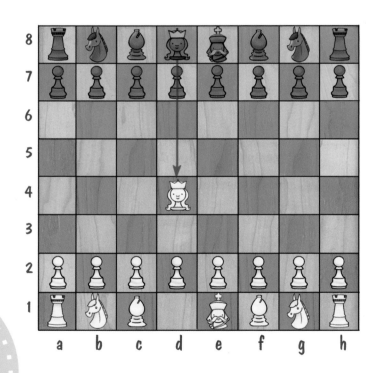

1 As you play you must always be on the lookout for long-range pieces hiding behind other pieces. White has just played her queen through the pawn in front to d4 but this is a bad choice! What can Black do now? That's right, all he has to do is play his own queen through his own pawn to capture her. Oops!

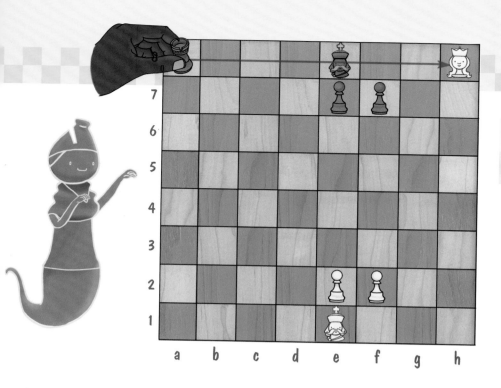

2 Ghost chess forces you to be flexible by turning around all those situations that you have become used to. Now you must look at the whole board and make use of every piece. What is the best way to get out of check here? The black rook takes the white queen, of course, and the king doesn't have to move!

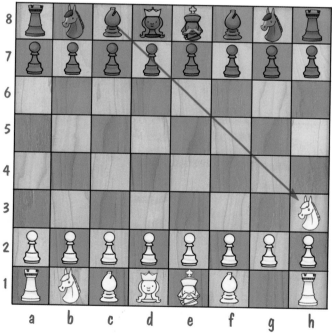

3 The knight on h3 could be taken by the bishop but would it be wise to take it? It would turn out to be an even trade, with the bishop being taken immediately by the pawn, bishop, or rook. You must decide if you want to lose a Ghost of your own.

4 Remember, you can't go through your opponent's pieces, otherwise you could make checkmate on move one! If you could go through any piece, then Black couldn't even block this check. Have a scary fun time with Ghost Chess on your own board now!

Triangle Forks

In chess, when you attack more than one piece or square at a time, it is called a **fork** or a **double attack**. Usually when you make a fork, the pieces form a triangle from which only one piece can escape. Here you'll see how many different types of triangles you can make with certain pieces. If you play with a partner, whoever gets the most triangles wins!

About this activity

Creating forks or double attacks is a tactic that will help you win material, as only one piece will be able to move out of the way at a time.

This is an activity you can do by yourself or in any partnership or group. You will need your chess set and a piece of paper and pencil so you can write down or draw the triangles you've made (see Tip, below). A ruler might be helpful, too!

If you're working by yourself, see how many different types of triangles you can make with the pieces suggested in the steps.

With a partner, you can work together to find triangles and write down your answers. You could also compete by playing independently with a timer. Whoever has more triangles wins.

Top tip

Why not use this activity to practice your chess notation (see page 60), too? Instead of drawing or describing each triangle, write them down in notation, e.g. Black: Be5; White: Rb2 Rh2

1 The best pieces at making forks are queens and knights, because they are the only two pieces that can move in eight different directions! Try to get them in the center of the board, so that they have the highest number of places to go!

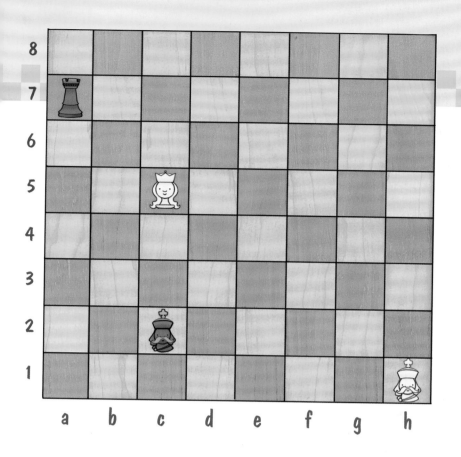

2 When you attack two pieces, only one can save itself at a time so you'll usually be able to capture the other one, free! The white queen has the king in check but is also aiming at the rook. When the king moves away, the rook is still there to be taken.

3 What's super-cool about forks, though, besides winning tons of stuff, is that you are also making a triangle with almost every one! Because you'll be using three pieces, those will be the three corners of a triangle. Some of the triangles might look funny, but they're there! Here's an example with a black bishop and two white rooks.

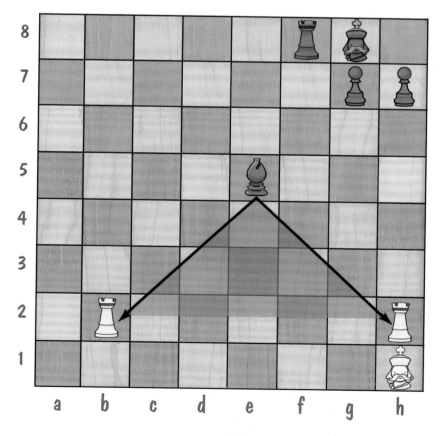

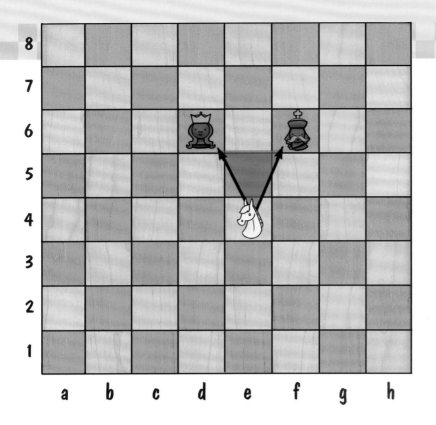

4 Start by using only knights to attack queens and kings. Place the black king on the board anywhere you like to start. Then add the white knight, creating a position that puts the king in check. Where would the black queen have to be, so that you'd attack her, too? Add her to the board and place her under attack by the knight. What you've created is a triangle! Do you see it?

5 Now keep going! Place the king, queen, and knight anywhere around the board, to make different types of triangles. Note that the triangles do NOT have to follow an exact path of straight squares along the board.

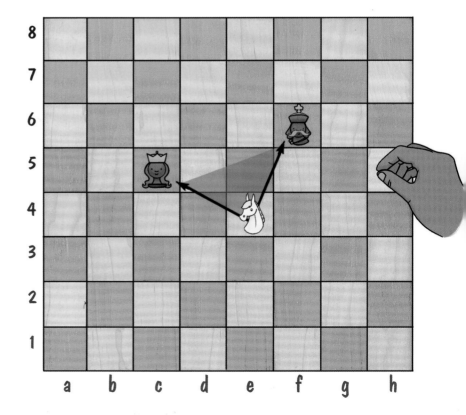

6 You might notice a trick is to use symmetry to find another answer! (This example is the same as the last one flipped over!) Which knight fork cannot use symmetry to create another one? (The solution is below.) Chess is so cool! Who knew there was so much fun math in chess? There's geometry, arithmetic, and even algebra! You must be some sort of genius! Learn this pattern well, because it is the foundation of many other tactics!

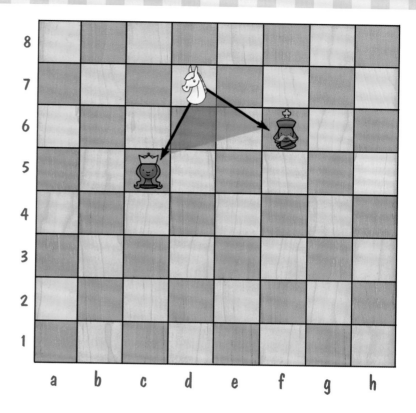

7 Now try the same activity but with queens attacking rooks and knights.

Variations

You can have different types of competitions. What's the biggest triangle you can make? How fast can you do it? Use any pieces you want to make the attacks—all pieces can create forks.

Solution to 6:
White: Ne5; Black: Qc4, Kg6

Remove the Guard

During a game your pieces can be used to protect one another, all working together to keep each other safe. Your queen may be guarding a bishop on the other side of the board, as well as a couple of pawns close by, but in this activity, if you lose your queen, you'll lose them, too! This tactic requires a bit of planning, because you do have to see two moves in a row. That's called a combination: when you do something so that something else occurs. Two tactics in a row! Remove the guard, then capture a **hanging piece**!

About this activity

You will need to set up your board as normal, and work with a partner. Keep concentrating, because the pieces will come off the board quickly in this game!

You will play a "regular" game of chess but if you can capture a piece that was guarding another piece, then you capture what it used to protect for free! As soon as someone makes a capture, you capture all the pieces that piece was protecting so you could take a lot of pieces in one turn!

If you capture the king (which you can't do in regular chess), you win! There is no check or checkmate in this game, since the kings can come off the board. So if the king is in danger, no need to announce, "Check!"

1 Remove the Guard is a tactic that highlights how pieces work together. In chess you would like to capture as much free stuff as possible. So to play defense, you need to protect your pieces, and to play offense, you need to prevent your opponent from protecting his/her pieces! You see where I'm going? Chess is fun because, just like in tennis, there is a lot of back and forth: sometimes you play defense, and sometimes you play offense, and sometimes you play both at the same time!

2 Another good time to use this tactic is when you are planning a checkmate. Let's say you are playing as Black and your queen is aiming at h2. It'd be fantastic if only you could make the move Qxh2 and checkmate the king! He wouldn't be able to capture her because of the helping bishop. But, wait! The knight on f3 is guarding the checkmate square—he could capture the queen if she landed on h2—so, before you can move your queen, you must remove the guard by capturing the knight with your rook on f8! When he's gone, you can checkmate on h2 as planned. You don't mind losing a rook to a pawn because, with the checkmate, you win the game!

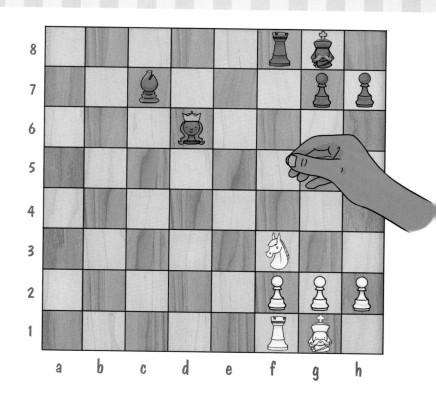

3 Now to play the game of Remove the Guard. Set up your board as normal and begin playing a game, but look out for opportunities to "remove the guard." In this game can you see that the bishop on b5 is attacking the knight? And what is the knight protecting? If you capture it, you can also remove the pieces it's guarding at the same time, so the black queen and the pawn on e5 also leave the board! Brutal!

Soon you will become aware that you are looking at the whole board to see who is protecting what. This way your pieces will work together harmoniously and your planning skills will definitely increase, too! If a piece gets removed, that might mean another piece from across the board could come out all of a sudden. Have fun with this one!

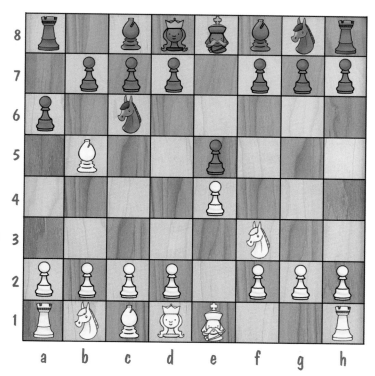

Pawns vs. the Queen

This game makes your pieces work with each other to help you practice making **double attacks** (see page 70) and playing **endgames** (when most pieces are off the board). In an endgame, your main goal is getting a pawn promoted—so here, if you're playing as the pawns, you win if one gets to the other side. The pawns work together to do this. If you're playing as the queen, you have to capture all the pawns to win—and you will use double attacks to achieve this.

About this activity

When you are playing as the pawns, you win if one of them can reach the other side, even if it can be captured that move! So long as it touches the other side, you win. If a queen can capture all eight pawns, then, of course, she will win. Who would you rather be?

You can play this activity by yourself or with a partner.

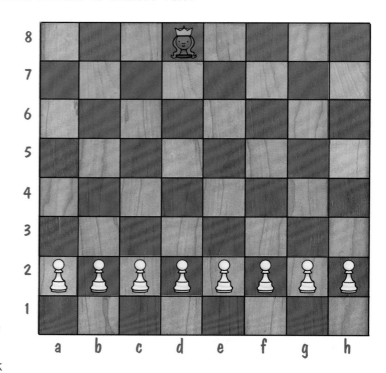

1 The queen's big job is to attack and eat everyone as fast as possible. She will look for **forks** to poke the pawns with. Her strength is the ability to look in all directions. But is that good enough?

The pawns need each other. With only one pawn pushing forward to become a queen, he will soon be eaten up. If there are two pawns, then it will take the queen a little longer, because she'll have to aim at the **hanging** (undefended) pawn first. (See page 83 to practice identifying hanging or protected pieces.)

2 You need eight white pawns and the black queen for this game. Start the pawns on their home rank. Start the queen on her home square (d8).

3 Do you think the queen is fast enough, or are the pawns faster? One example of how this game could go would be for a white pawn to move forward to d3, then Black plays Qd4, aiming at b2 and f2 (a fork!). She wouldn't want to capture on d3, because either the c2 or e2 pawn would simply take her back.

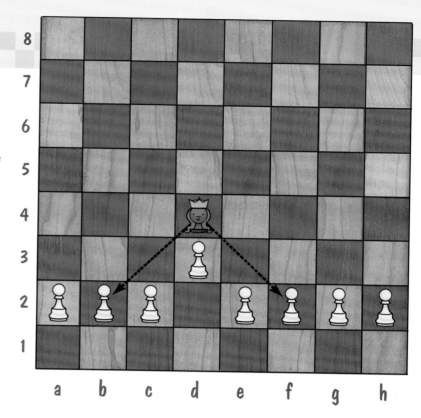

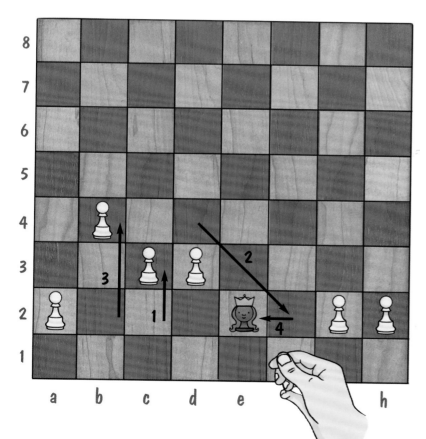

4 Follow the numbered arrows, moving the pieces on your own chessboard, to see how this game progresses from the position in step 3. First, a pawn moves forward to c3, blocking one of the queen's attacks, but she goes the other way anyway and takes the pawn at f2. The b-pawn makes a run for the far rank and moves to b4, but the queen counters by taking the pawn at e2.

5 The a-pawn is now in danger, so he moves forward to a4, but this leaves the first pawn at d3 open to attack by the queen. After the queen takes the d-file pawn, the pawn at b4 moves forward to b5, only for the queen to take the pawn at c3.

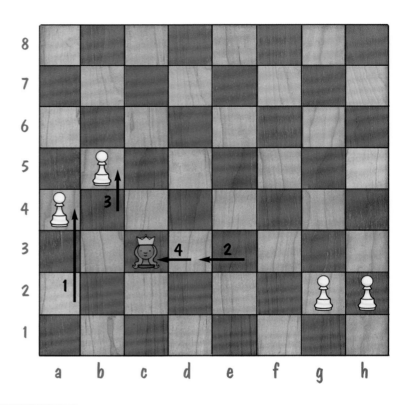

6 The b-pawn moves forward again to b6 and the queen gives chase to b4. Now she's in a position to take two pieces again, either a4 or b6— another fork!

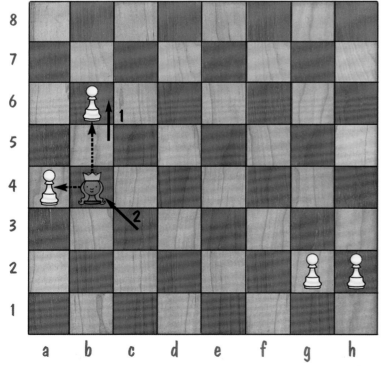

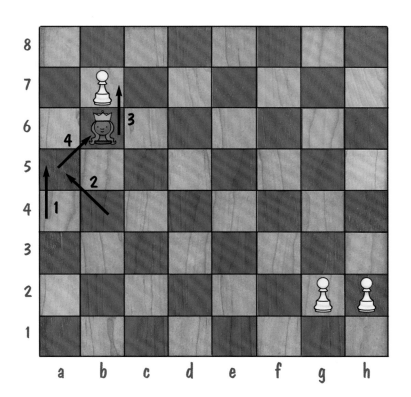

Notation

If you write down the moves from this game, as we learned in Team Chess (see page 60), it would look like this:

1. d3 Qd4
2. c3 Qxf2
3. b4 Qxe2
4. a4 Qxd3
5. b5 Qxc3
6. b6 Qb4
7. a5 Qxa5
8. b7 Qb6
9. b8=Q (the "=" means that the pawn promotes to a queen—and in this activity, wins!)

Always write down the moves as you go along—it'll help you remember each game you've played.

7 The a-pawn moves from a4 to a5, and the queen then captures him, landing on a5. This means the pawn at b6 has the chance to move forward again. Now he's ahead, nothing can stop him getting to the back rank. Pawns win! What should the queen have done to ensure a different outcome? (See solution below.)

Variations

Try playing this activity with a white queen and black pawns. Look at the difference between having a white queen and a black queen. If you have a white queen, she goes first, so what will she do automatically? Start capturing pawns! And if the pawns are white and go first, they will defend themselves first. So it is harder for Black in both cases, do you see why? This means, in your regular games of chess, you should be attacking with White!

Another variation you could try is five pawns vs. a rook (make sure the pawns stay together or it will be very hard for them!). Don't neglect your little pawns—they can turn into a super-powerful queen more often than you think!

Solution to 7:
If the queen had captured the pawn on b6 rather than the one on a4, the pawn on a4 couldn't move without being captured, so White would have to try to get the pawns on g2 and h2 to the other side—tricky when they're both still on their home squares!

Trap the Queen

☺☺◯

"Pins" and "skewers" are two common and very helpful tactics to learn. Pins are used to keep something in place in the real world—it's the same with chess! If you pin an opponent's piece, it can't, or shouldn't, move! A skewer is like an X-ray—it can see through one piece to the next. Check out the different types, then see if you can trap the queen.

About this activity

For pins and skewers, you always have three pieces in a straight line. Which pieces go really far in straight lines? The long-range pieces: queens, rooks, and bishops. So these are the only pieces that can make pins and skewers.

Check out the examples to learn how to make them, then try the Trap the Queen puzzle. It's a famous, amazing position: everywhere the queen goes, she is trapped by another piece with a pin or a skewer!

You could work out the puzzle on your own or with a friend. Once you've solved it, why not set it up for other friends or your parents? Challenge them to find a safe place for the queen!

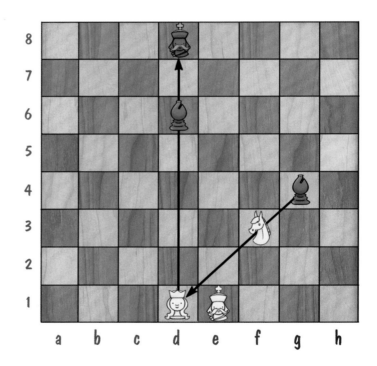

1 There are two kinds of pins in chess: the **absolute pin** and the **relative pin**. An absolute pin is when the king is behind the pinned piece. Here, the bishop on d6 is completely and absolutely pinned. It might want to go to b4 and say check, but it can't. That would be illegal as it would leave the black king in check by the white queen, and you can never put your own king in danger!

A relative pin means that you could move the piece, but it would be a really bad idea. Do you see what would happen if the white knight on f3 moved away in the position above?

2

White can make seven different pins on Black on this board—can you find all of them?

The absolute pins are Raf1, Rgf1, Bc4, and Ra7. The relative pins are Rae1, Rge1, and Bh4.

(Did you find Ra6, too? That one doesn't really count, because both attacked pieces—the two knights—are worth less than the rook attacking them and are defended by the king and queen.)

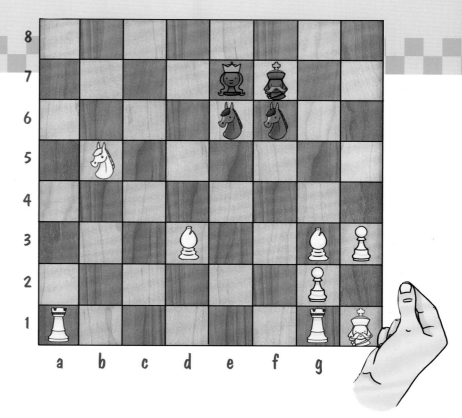

3

In this puzzle, there are lots of pinned pieces! It's White's turn, and the black pieces can only watch sorrowfully as White slides the rook to h8 with checkmate. No one can capture back! Notice that White's bishop on b3 is pinned, too (an absolute pin).

Top tip

Often you don't want to capture a pinned piece at all—sometimes you can make it stay there for life, while it watches helplessly, as you create a checkmate or capture another piece for free. If the pinned piece is guarded, and you won't win material, don't capture it. Instead, sometimes it's better to attack it again with another piece—put pressure on it! Think of "pp on the pp": "put pressure on the pinned piece."

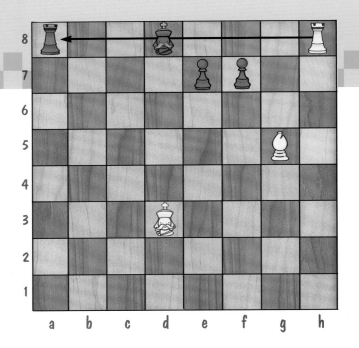

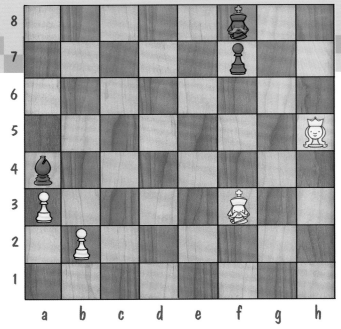

4 Skewers are similar to pins, but the more valuable piece is in front of the less valuable piece. You still have three pieces in the same straight line. Here, the white rook on h8 is creating a skewer, because when the black king moves (he must because he is in check), the white rook will capture the black rook for free (without anyone capturing him back).

White also has an absolute pin on the pawn at e7 at this point.

5 You have Black. Let's see if you can make a skewer in the following position. (The solution is on page 126.)

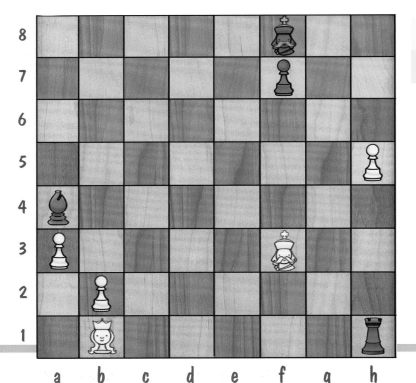

6 Now, are you ready for the super-tricky puzzle? Set up your board exactly as shown. Your job is to look at all the possible escape squares for the white queen. Then, find out why each of them loses the queen!

The cleverest place the queen might hide is h7, but even this doesn't work! Look at what happens—follow these moves on your board:

1. Qh7 Rxh5
2. Qxh5 Bd1+

If she doesn't capture the rook on move 2, she will run into all the other pins and skewers!

Did you find all the rest of the pins and skewers? The answers are on page 126.

Hanging & Capturing Game

In this activity you must capture as many **hanging pieces** as you can. Checkmate still wins, but this game will go more quickly because more pieces come off the board each time you capture a hanging piece.

About this activity

- - - - - - - - - - - - - - - -

In this game we learn to identify hanging pieces—pieces that are undefended. We also learn a tactic called **hanging**, which is about capturing pieces and not letting your own pieces get captured in return.

This game is for two players.

1 Before you start the game, practice identifying hanging pieces. A hanging piece is one that is undefended and can be captured for free. If there are a lot of pieces attacking and defending a certain piece, you have two ways of figuring out if it's hanging or protected. You can visualize the possible moves, for example, you think: he goes here, I capture, he captures, I capture, he captures, then I capture back…

But you can also simply count the attackers aiming at the piece and the defenders protecting the piece.

2 If the number of attackers is greater than the number of defenders, the piece is hanging. Here, if it's Black's turn, Black will come out on top as there are two pieces attacking the pawn on e4 but only only one white pawn defending it.

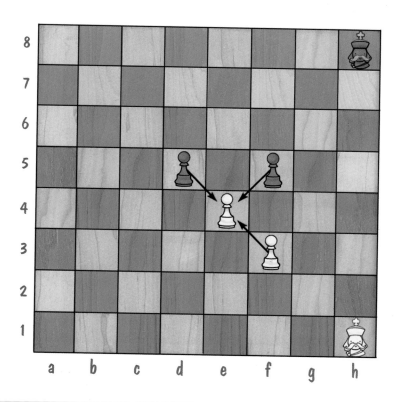

3 If the number of attackers and defenders is equal, the piece is protected. Look again at the pawn on e4. Here it is protected because Black cannot take it out without being taken tit for tat.

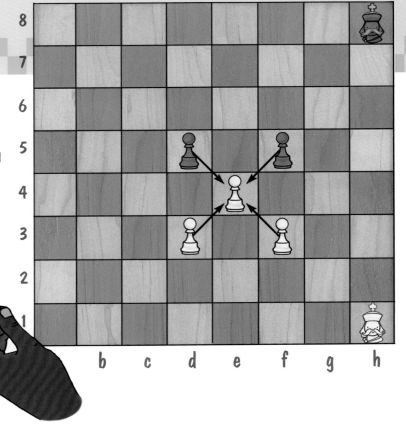

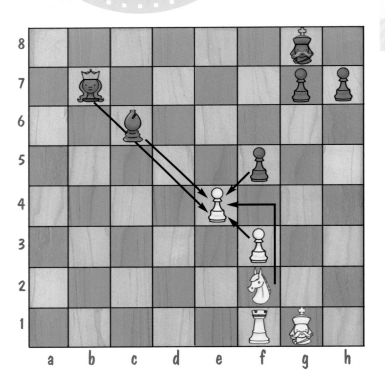

4 Visualizing what will happen next in chess is not that easy. You can practice and improve at this skill, but counting is a great alternative. Remember to include pieces that "look through" another piece going in the same direction, as they are are counted, too—once the first piece moves out of the way, the piece behind it will help attack/defend.

Think about counting like playing basketball: it's 3 on 2. Whose team would you rather be on? How many pieces are now attacking the pawn on e4 and how many are defending it?

Can you work out what will happen if Black takes the pawn? Follow these moves on your board:

    1. ...fxe4

    2. fxe4 Bxe4

    3. Nxe4 Qxe4

White has won a bishop and a pawn, but Black has won a knight and two pawns.

How to play the game

If you **trade** pieces with your opponent (you capture one of their pieces, they capture back a piece of equal value), nothing unusual happens.

If you capture a hanging (undefended) piece, you can immediately take another piece of equal value off the board. So, if you capture a pawn for free, you can take off another pawn from anywhere you want.

If you capture a piece of higher value, even though you are taken straight back, you can take pieces off the board that add up to the difference between your piece and your opponent's. So if one of your pawns captures your opponent's rook and then your pawn gets captured straight after, you can take off pieces worth four points (five points for the rook minus one point for the pawn equals four points).

This game will continue until one side has lost all the material possible (besides the king!). At that time, checkmate should be very near!

The values of each piece are given below (see also Capturing Game, page 27). Remember that kings never get captured, only checkmated!

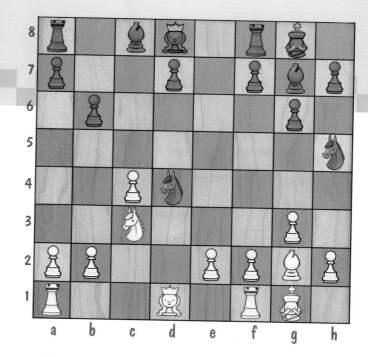

5 Now try playing a game! Here's an example, shown halfway through a game, to show how the scoring works. White could play the bishop to a8 and take the rook without anyone capturing him back. The rook is worth five points so now you can take off pieces that also add up to five: the other rook, or five pawns, or perhaps a bishop and two pawns.

6 "Hanging" may also refer to winning material, as in, for example, capturing something more valuable, even if you get captured back. Here, the white knight on c6, worth three points, can take the black queen, worth nine points. Although the knight will get captured straight after by the king, this is still a good move, because White can take off pieces totaling six points (nine minus three) when it captures the queen.

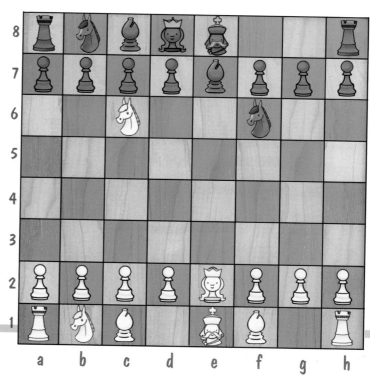

Scholar's Mate

Now that you've started learning tactics, you also need to discover some special tricks that will help you actually win a game. There are some combinations of moves that will take you straight through to checkmate if your opponent isn't concentrating, and the Scholar's Mate is a four-move checkmate that every beginner chess player should know. You may not win with it every time, but it can astound adults when you beat them in less than a minute!

About this activity

Checkmate is how you win a chess game, and this is one of the fastest ways to get there. If you use one piece alone, it could be captured. With two pieces, one will protect the other. The queen is the best at making checkmate, and here, the bishop will protect her. Remember that you can never put your own king in danger, so he may not capture a protected piece.

You need a chess set but not necessarily a partner! You can work by yourself, or you can work with one or two other people to discover the checkmate. When you practice it, you should play with one other person.

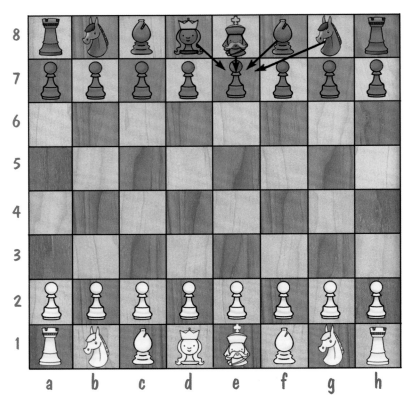

1 Each square is strong or weak, depending on the number of pieces that defend it. f7 is extremely weak, because only the king is able to take the piece that lands on it. On the other hand, e7, just next door, is extremely strong because four pieces—the knight, the bishop, the queen, and the king—defend it.

2 So to make checkmate, you are going to use your queen and bishop to aim at f7. First, try by yourself to discover where your white queen and light-squared bishop could move to attack and aim at f7. Don't give Black any moves for this game. How many moves did it take you?

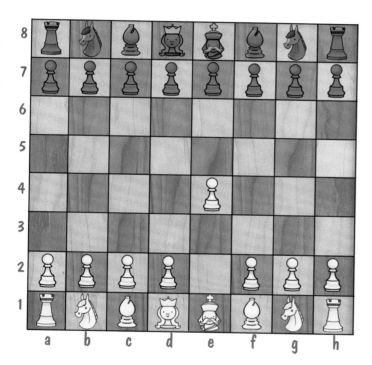

3 Did you succeed in getting checkmate? Let's go through it together. Your first move allows the queen and bishop to develop so that they can both aim at the weakest square on the board, f7. First, bring out your white king's pawn. That's pawn to e4. This is a great first move, even if you don't decide to do the Scholar's Mate! It attacks the center of the board (which is the most important—see Center Points, page 93), and allows the queen and bishop to develop right away if they want to. We are only going to look at White's moves at first.

4 Next, get out your queen to h5. (There are different ways of achieving the same result, so if you got a different second move, that's okay.) She is looking at two pawns, and three if we imagine Black has played e5. But she is most interested in the weak pawn on f7.

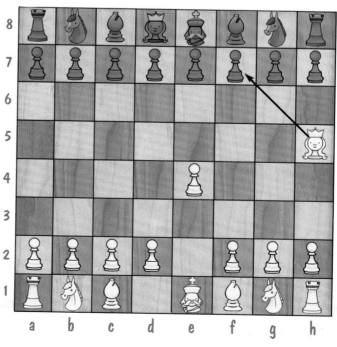

5 Remember, the queen cannot do it alone; she needs a helper. Now bring out your bishop to c4. From here he attacks f7! Now we have two attackers on f7! And Black still only has the one king defending. Two is bigger than one so we are ready to capture it and say, "Checkmate!"

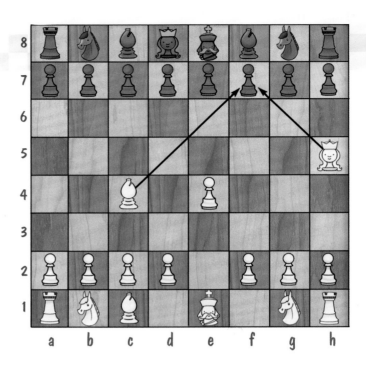

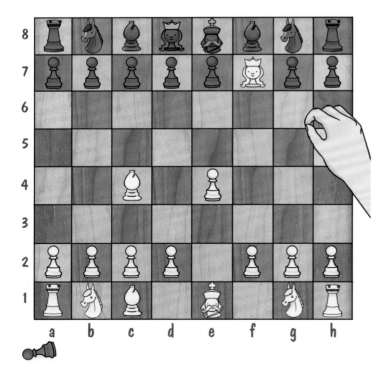

6 Use your queen to take the pawn on f7! The black king may not capture her back, because that would be an illegal move: the bishop would then put the king in danger—so, checkmate, because the king cannot move, block, or capture to escape!

Variations

Try to discover how to stop this threat if you are Black. If someone tries this checkmate on you, you should know how to stop it! Start from Move 3 in step 7, but take back the knight from f6. Try to find a better move that will block the queen's path… (The solution is on page 126.)

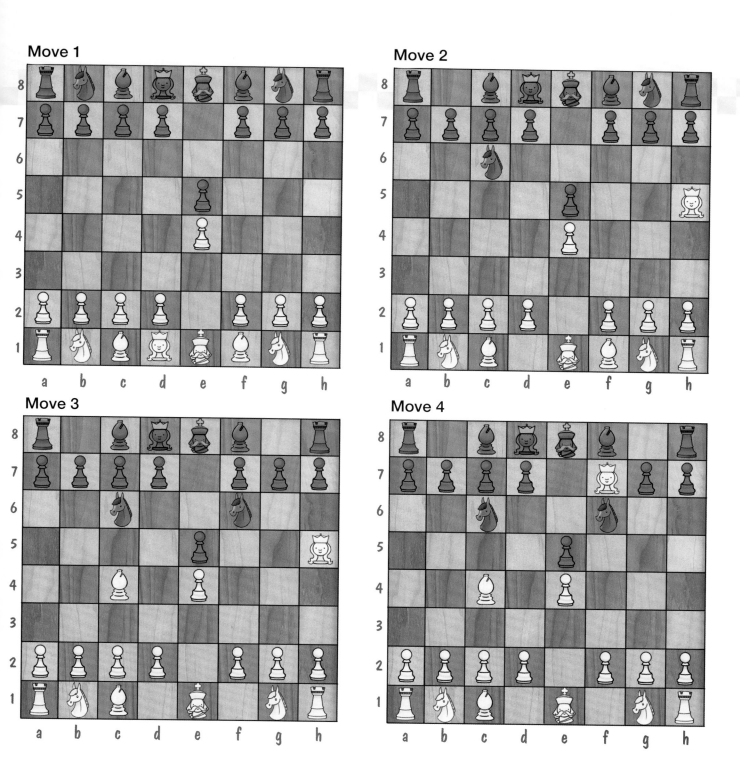

Move 1

Move 2

Move 3

Move 4

7 Now let's add Black's moves to see the whole thing. First, he would counter with his king's pawn to e5, but that doesn't worry us. After the queen is brought out to h5, he would likely play his knight to c6 to guard the hanging pawn on e5, and follow our bishop to c4 with his other knight to f6 to attack the queen. But she's not staying there! We move our queen to f7, capture the pawn, and say "Checkmate!"

Create-a-Discovery

Another great tactic is the "discovered attack," or "discovery," for short. The idea is that after you move one piece, it is the piece behind it that is making the attack. Practice these discoveries, then try to create them yourself.

About this activity

The discovered attack gives you a great chance to capture while your opponent's trying to stay in the game. If you can use the move to take one of his pieces, you'll be ahead of him in material, and with more material, you are more likely to win the game.

Setting up this move requires you to look at the whole board, because it involves your long-range pieces (queens, rooks, and bishops). Do you remember what they are good at? (See Trap the Queen, page 80.)

Work by yourself or with a partner and use any long-range piece to make the attack, along with any piece in between, so long as there isn't a check when you start out.

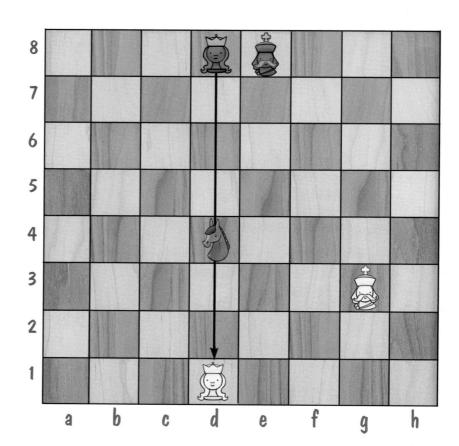

1 When three pieces are lined up, with the queen, bishop, or rook at the back, all you have to do is move the piece in the middle, and the piece behind it makes the attack.

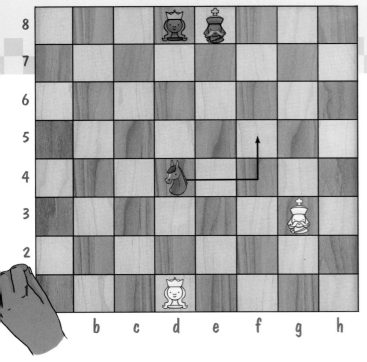

2 This is a "discovered attack"—when the piece behind another (in this case, the black queen, which is behind the black knight) aims at any piece except the king. The knight moves and the white queen discovers she is under attack from the black queen. But, because the king is now in check by the knight on f5, he must move (so the queen cannot move)! On the next turn, after the king gets out of danger, the black queen will capture the white queen for free.

3 In this example, we have switched the positions of the white queen and king. Black will do the same move, but here it's called a "discovered check"—the piece behind aims at the king. The black knight can move out of the way, anywhere, and the queen is the one giving check. The best place for the knight is f5 because, similar to last time, the white king must move out of check, and then the knight captures the queen. (If White tries to block the check by moving the queen to d3, rather than moving the king, then the black queen will still capture her!)

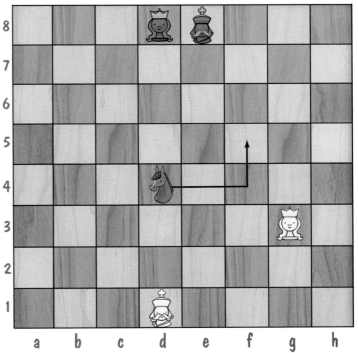

4 Now you try! Create a position where you could make a discovered attack in a single move. Start out with the four pieces you want to use, two white and two black. Line up three of the pieces: put the piece that makes the attack at the back, a different piece in the middle (the one to move), and an opposing piece at the front. Can you do it?

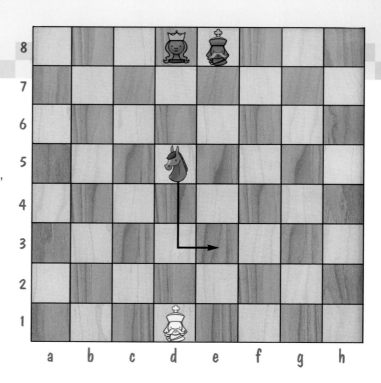

5 A third discovery is the discovered double check! This is the most powerful kind of check. Instead of three ways to get out (move, block, capture), the king is left with just one: move! That's because since two pieces are attacking the king, capturing or blocking one isn't enough! Here, the black knight moves to e3, so now both he and the queen have the white king in check.

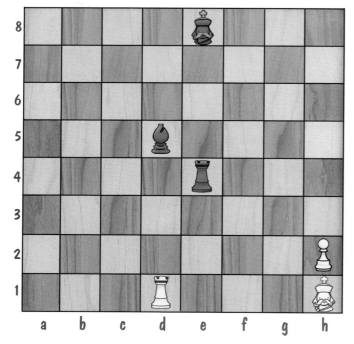

6 Double check is very useful for checkmate. Here, it's Black's turn— what would you do? (The answer is on page 126.)

Variations

You can challenge yourself by using a timer, or setting up a tough puzzle for your friends to solve. You can see how many puzzles you can create in five minutes, and compare that to a friend. The more you practice this tactic, the more likely you are to be able to find this pattern in a real game!

Center Points

The four really important squares for your pawns and pieces to control are right in the center: d4, d5, e4, and e5. From here you have way more possible moves than if you move toward the side of the board and that can only be a good thing. This game places a value on reaching the center squares as well as capturing pieces.

About this activity

In this game, if you reach one of the center squares, you earn **ten points**. If you position a piece so that it can reach a center square on your next go, you get **five points**. Castling is also worth **ten points**.

You should play moves that allow your pieces to move toward the middle. Everything can still capture, so don't drop a piece in the middle if it can get taken!

After seven moves, whoever has more points wins. Count up the pieces captured—they are worth the same value as usual (see page 27 for a reminder)—and the points you got from aiming at the center. You also get a bonus **ten points** for each piece left in a center square at the end.

Play with a partner! You need your chess set and a pencil and paper to keep track of points.

see page 27 for a reminder

Top tip

The most important part of the board at the beginning of a game is the center. Your strategy for the opening should always be "C, D, C"—meaning "center, develop, castle." If you can develop your pieces toward the center and also be in a position to castle (see page 50), you will gain a huge advantage.

(see page 50)

1 When you play Center Points, always look to the center. In this example, the knight has moved to h3 on move one so, on his next turn, he can continue to two squares: g5 or f4 (or back home). White has made a bad choice—he is nowhere near the center!

2 If instead the knight had gone to f3 on move one, he would've been able to choose from four squares: d4, e5, g5, or h4 (or back home)—and two of those are in the center. That's twice as many options! In chess, the more choices your pieces have, the more flexible you can be with your plans, and the more likely one of them will be a good choice.

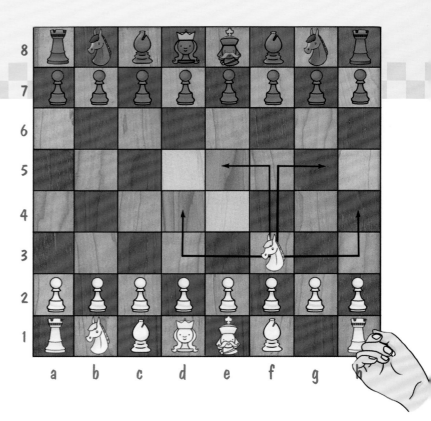

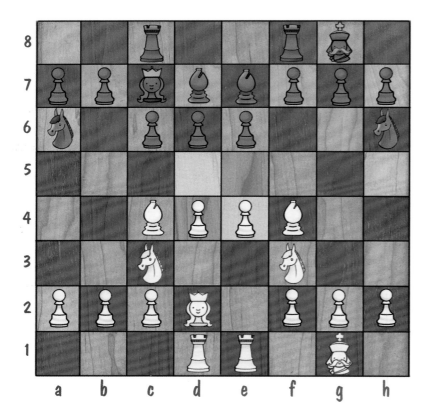

3 Here's another example. The center squares are so crucial that people will actually say one side is winning simply if they have "control" over the center. In this early position, White has control: two of her pawns are in the center squares and they are defending the other two center squares (that is, if a black piece moves onto them, the pawns can capture it). The white bishops and knights are also defending the other two center squares!

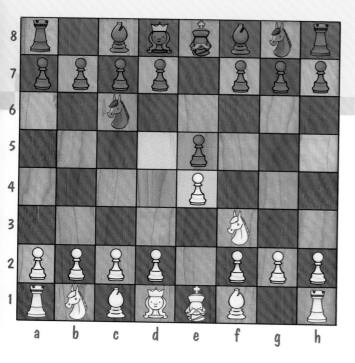

 Now let's play the game!
Right now both sides have
made two moves and
gained 15 points: no pieces
have been taken but each has a pawn
in the center (ten points) and a knight
aiming at the center (five points).

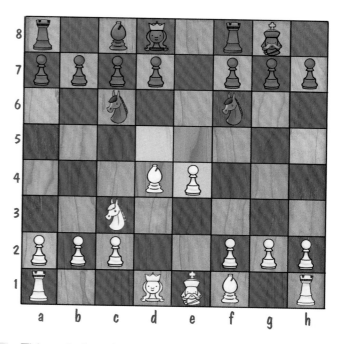

Variations

You can play this
game in a number
of different ways.
You can eliminate
the bonus points,
or change the
number of points
won. You can add
another ring around
the center and
give one or two
points for landing
here. The goal is
that you are able
to recognize the
importance of
the center in the
beginning of a
chess game.

 This notation shows how the game progresses
and when each player gets points. Follow the
moves on your board and, by the end, you should
have the positions shown here.

1. e4 (10: center)   e5 (10: center)
2. Nf3 (5: aim at center)   Nc6 (5: aim at center)
3. d4 (10: center)   exd4 (10: center + 1: capture)
4. Nxd4 (10: center + 1: capture)   Nf6 (5: aim at center)
5. Nc3 (5: aim at center)   Bc5 (5: aim at center)
6. Be3 (5: aim at center)   Bxd4 (10: center + 3: capture)
7. Bxd4 (10: center + 3: capture)   0-0 (10: castling)
PLUS 20 bonus points (2 x 10:
two pieces left in center)

Totals: White 79—Black 59
White wins! Now you try!

Chapter 4
Planning & Checkmates

The Queen Dance

The queen is my favorite piece. Because she can move in eight different directions, she is perfect for creating checkmates. When you're at the end of a chess game and you have just your queen and king against a king, there is a really simple pattern to trap and checkmate the king. The queen can ALMOST do it herself, but she does need the help of her king. This activity shows you how.

About this activity

If you're left with a queen and a king against a solitary king, you can use this technique to win the game—just make sure you know how to dance!

Use a chess set and play this activity by yourself or with a partner.

Top tip

Sometimes you can look at a position and think that there's no way to win, but often there's a simple pattern for getting to checkmate!

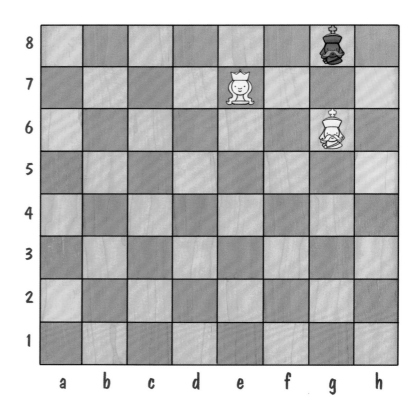

1 To see how easy it is to use just the queen, first see if you can find three different checkmates here. That's right, moving the queen to d8, e8, or g7 will create checkmate. To get into this position during a game is simple: we do the Queen Dance! Do you know how to waltz?

2 Let's get into dancing position. We need to start by first trying to get our queen a knight's distance away from the opposing king. (Psst! The queen does not MOVE like a knight, of course!)

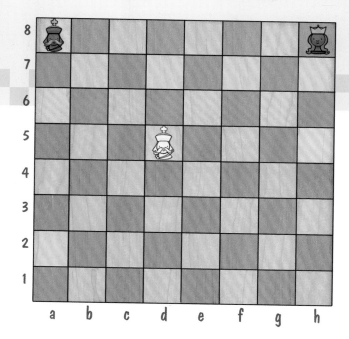

3 The queen has two options from h8—she can move to f6 or c3 to get a knight's distance away from the king. Let's move her to f6.

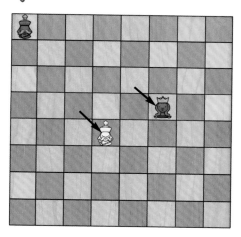

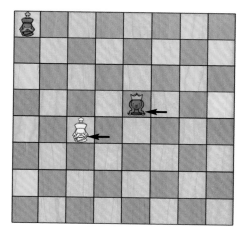

4 Now she's ready to boogie—wherever the king goes, the queen follows! On every move, she's always a knight's distance away from the king. If the king moves one step to the left, the queen follows.

Here he moves to c5 and the queen moves to e6. If he moves one square diagonally down to the right, the queen does exactly the same thing. Follow the arrows to see how the queen dances!

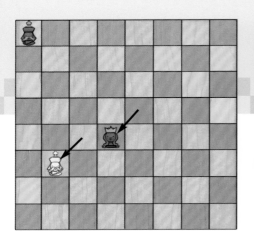
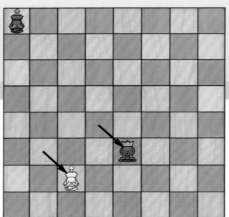
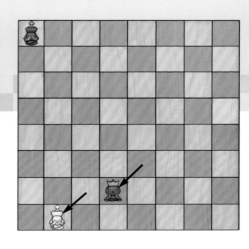

5 Notice how the queen hasn't put the king in check. Sometimes, if we just check the king all day, it will get very tiring, and we will get a draw. Do you want a draw, or do you want to win?! Well, if you have the king and the queen, you will probably want to win, so do this Queen Dance until you can make checkmate!

6 Slowly, the queen is trapping the king. He is going closer and closer to the corner, and there is nothing that he can do about it! This is a really easy pattern to remember. Keep going until the king has nowhere to go except right in the corner!

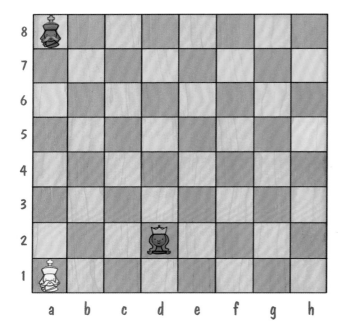

7 Red flashing lights! You have to stop dancing now because otherwise you'll end up in a **stalemate**. Remember that a stalemate is when no piece can move, but the king is not in check, and the game ends in a draw. That'd be frustrating when you could so easily win!

8 Look what happens if you carry on dancing and move the queen to c2. If you do, the king will not be able to move anywhere without putting himself in check, so that's stalemate.

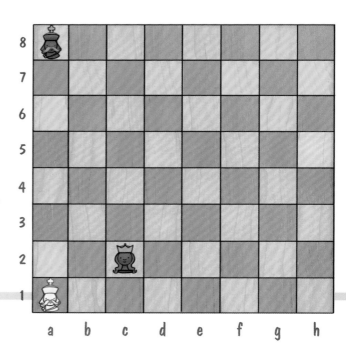

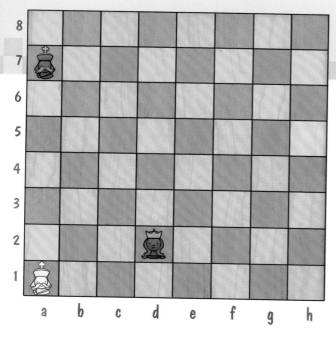

9

So, don't follow the king into the corner. Leave the queen where she is and start to bring in your king. The white king can move back and forth between a1 and b1: there's no escape for him but he won't be in stalemate, either.

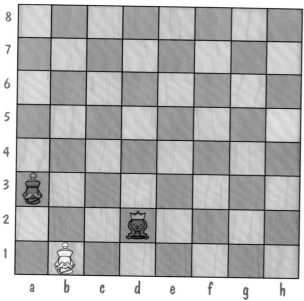

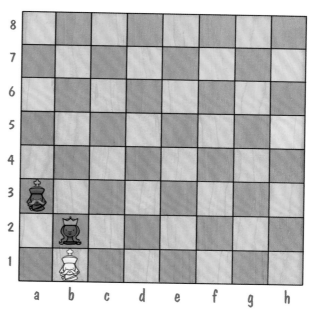

10 When the black king reaches a3, he's close enough to help. (Remember helper mates on page 45?) Place the queen on b2 and you will have put the king in a Sloppy Joe checkmate (also on page 45). How easy was that?

Let's review!

1. Get the queen a knight's distance away from the opposing king.

2. Start dancing! Wherever the king goes, the queen follows!

3. When the king touches the corner, red flashing lights should go off in your head: don't get into a stalemate, bring in the king to make checkmate!

4. When your king is close enough (remember, two kings never touch—they can never be next to each other), you should be able to get checkmate in one move!

Boots & Bug

Did you know that all you need to make a checkmate are two rooks? They simply trap the king at the edge of the board. Pretend your rooks are like feet. Really big feet in black boots! And there is this bug in your house (the king). But, you don't want to step on the bug, because that would be gross, and you don't want the bug to bite one of your toes. So somehow you have to shoo the bug out the window or out the front door without anyone getting hurt!

About this activity

Remember, checkmate means the king is in danger, and you cannot move, block, or capture to escape.

You can practice this checkmate by yourself, or with a partner. (Just make sure you both get a chance to be the boots!)

1 In this checkmate, you will use two black rooks to trap the white king at the edge of the board. Follow the pattern using your own chess set and board. Put your rooks on a8 and b7, and place the king on e5.

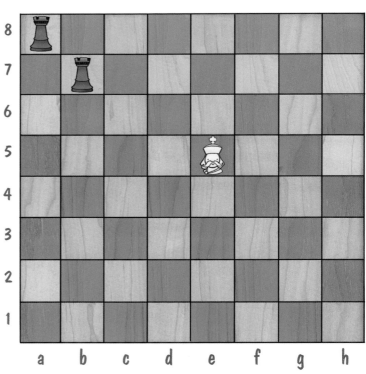

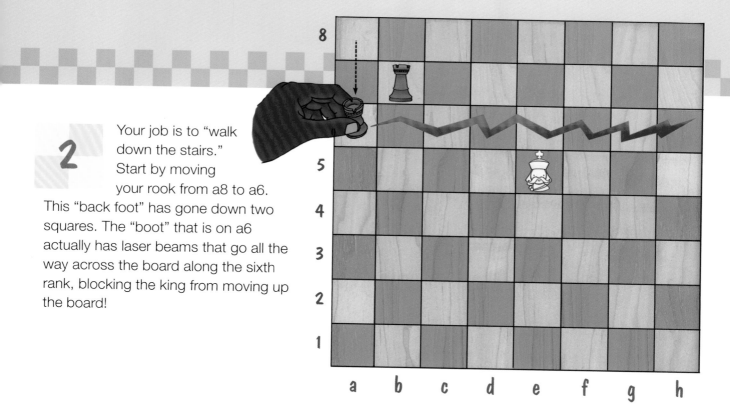

2 Your job is to "walk down the stairs." Start by moving your rook from a8 to a6. This "back foot" has gone down two squares. The "boot" that is on a6 actually has laser beams that go all the way across the board along the sixth rank, blocking the king from moving up the board!

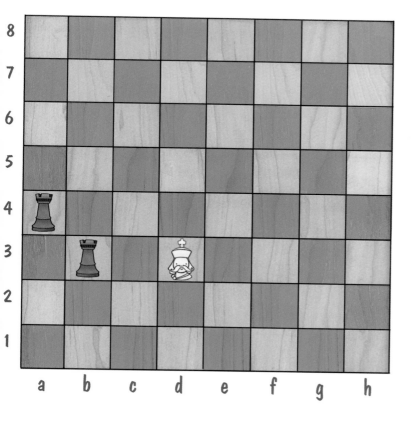

3 The king wants to get away from the laser beam, so he moves to e4. Next, move your other rook down two squares from b7 to b5 as he is now the "back foot." The king moves again to, say, d4 as he is now blocked from being on the fifth rank—those laser beams again!)

Black's turn. Bring your back foot down two steps from a6 to a4. Check! The king moves down again, to d3. Which foot should move now? The back foot, of course, on b5. And how many steps? Two! So play rook to b3 on your board, and say, "Check!" to the king.

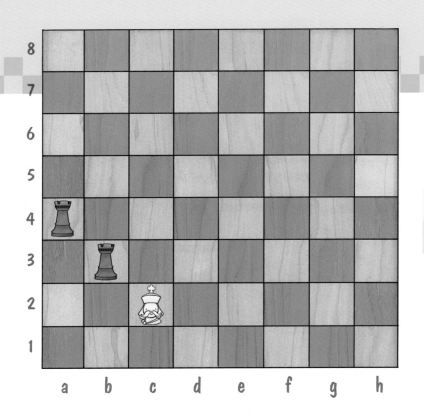

Top tip

You can also make this checkmate using a rook and a queen!

4 Danger! So far, the white king has been obliging in running straight down the board. But what if he gets close to your toes?! If he goes to c2 now, you'd better slow down!

5 He is getting ready to capture the foot on b3! It's time to do the splits! Take the foot on b3 and move it all the way across the board to h3 where he is safe from getting bitten by the bug. The king/bug is in between both feet now and you can continue pressing forward. Look down at him: this foot is safe, that foot is safe, the bug is safe—for now…

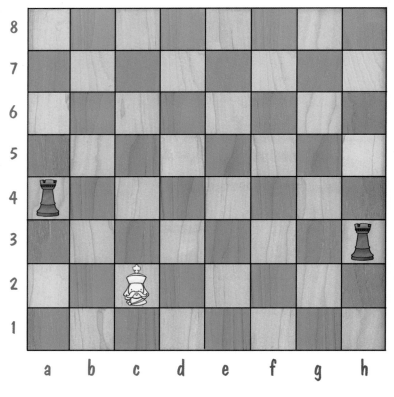

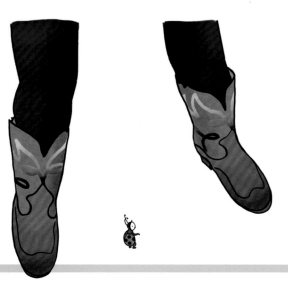

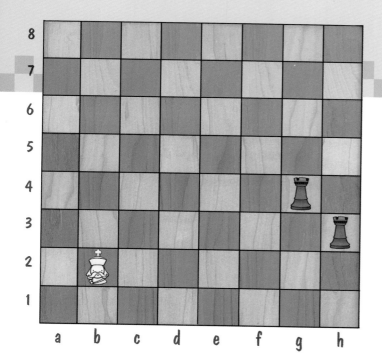

6 But what if the bug gets closer? Put the king on b2, so that if you were to bring the back foot down from a4 to a2, see ya later rookie! Ouch! Instead, bring your feet back together, but far away from the bug. (He doesn't have wings after all.) The rook on a4 goes to g4. Don't go to h4 because then you will be walking a tightrope! And it's very hard for big fat rooks to walk the tightrope.

7 With both rooks on the other side of the board they go back to "walking position." If the king goes to c2, trying to get closer, he will be too slow! Your back foot can easily come down the board without fear of getting bitten. So play rook to g2. Check! Laser beams force the king to the first rank—let's say c1!

Excellent: this is the moment you've been waiting for! You know which rook to move, right? Rook to h1 is checkmate! The king cannot move to either side because the rook on h1 is attacking every square along that first rank. And he can't move forward, because the rook on g2 attacks every square on the second rank, and the bug jumps out the door! Game over!

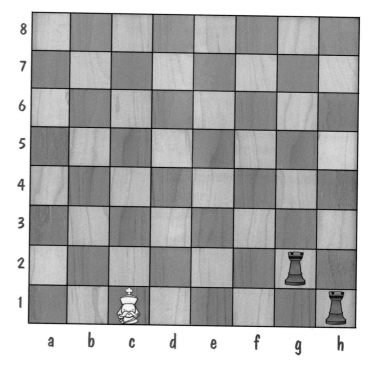

8 Now it's your turn! Practice this checkmate, starting from the position in step 1, so that you know how to use it if you get the chance in a game.

Dog on the Loose! ☺ ☺ ☺

In this checkmate, the king that you're trying to trap is like a dog running loose in your neighborhood. He's cute, but you can't really tackle him, so you must create an invisible fence around him and push him back until he's home. You do this with your rook and your king. This mate works a lot like the Queen Dance (see page 98)—rook and king slowly make the box around the other king smaller and smaller until... CHECKMATE!

About this activity

A rook is great at creating a back-rank mate—where the king is trapped at the back or front of the board—because he can guard an entire rank (horizontal line) on a chessboard. The rook can also guard a file (vertical line).

All you need for this mate is a rook and a king, and a king of the other color.

As with the other checkmates, practice this one on your own or with a friend.

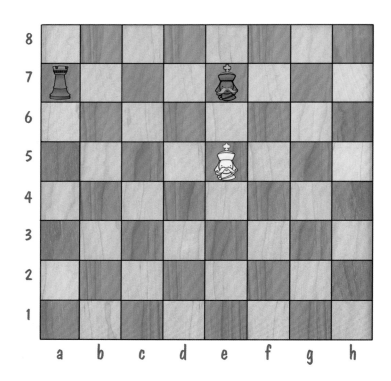

1 Let's see how to go about trapping the white king. Remember, he's like a loose dog—you can't just run up to him and catch him! You—your rook—need to herd him to where you want him, but it's tricky to do that on your own, so you need Dad—your king. That's the first step: getting your king and rook next to each other.

2
It's your (Black's) turn. You move your rook to d7—now you and your dad are teamed up! You have also already made a box around the white king!

3
On each move ask yourself one question, "Can I make the box smaller (safely)?" If so, move your rook. If not, move your king. That's it!

4
The other thing to remember is that there are no checks. Just running around checking the king all day is quite tiring. In fact, it's probably going to be a draw if you just say check, check, check… and never checkMATE. It's like you and the dog are having a face-off, and you get in front of him, but then he runs to the side. So you get in front again, AHA! but then he trots to the other side. Pretty soon, you're going to get tired.

5
The white king moves to f5. Can Black make the box smaller, safely? Yes! The rook moves to d6.

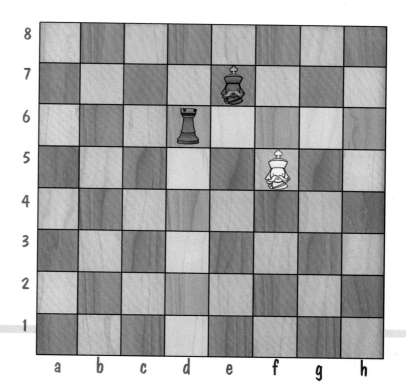

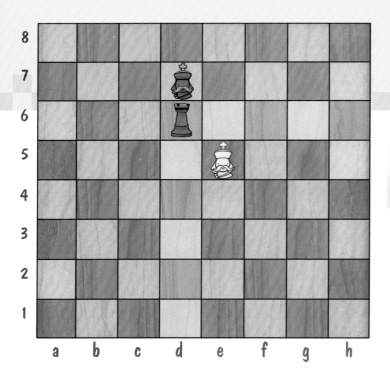

6 Next, White moves to e5. This time you can't move your rook because White has created opposition, so the black king has to move and goes to d7. This keeps the box tight and protects the rook from attack. (If the black king had moved to f7, White could have taken the unprotected rook on d6.)

7 When White moves to f5, it's safe for the rook to make the box smaller again—the rook moves to e6.

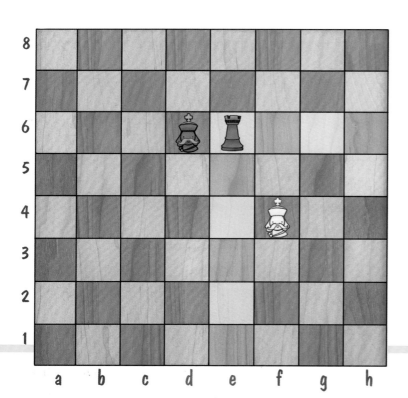

8 Now the white king moves to f4. Can the rook make the box smaller? No—if he moves to f6, he'll put the king in check, which lets the king out of the box. If he moves to e5 he could be captured. So the black king moves instead (to d6).

9 Let's continue. Keep asking if you can make the box smaller. If yes, move your rook. If no, bring in your king. If you're not sure where to put your king, try to make opposition! This will help you to keep pushing the opposing king into the corner.

10 Follow the next moves on your own board:
1. Kf5 Kd5
2. Kf4 Re5
3. Kf3 Re4
4. Kg3 Ke5
5. Kf2 Kf4
6. Kg1 Re2
7. Kh1

Great! Finally, that dog is back in his own yard.

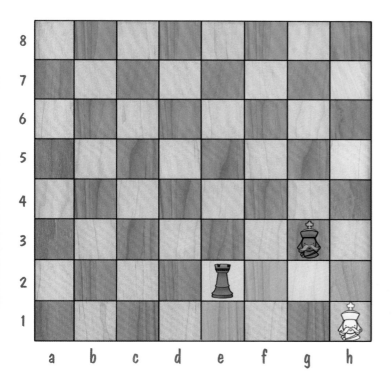

11 Now, how to keep him there? Checkmate will happen when your king gets a knight's move away from the corner. That way he guards all the doggie's escape squares. Once your king goes to g3, it's mate in one! (White can only move to g1, so the black rook moves to e1. Checkmate!)

Let's review!

1. Kings and rook work together (you need Dad's help).

2. Ask yourself (in your head, not out loud), "Can I make the box smaller safely?"

3. Answer (in your head!): Yes. Then make the box smaller. No, then bring in the king. (And try for opposition.)

4. When the dog/king is in the corner, get your king a knight's move away from the corner. And don't let me catch you moving the king like a knight.

5. CHECKMATE! (No stalemates, please.) The end! Go for it on your own board!

Double Bishops

Now you are ready to learn a super-hard checkmate using only two bishops! It's impossible to make checkmate with only one bishop—it will always be an automatic draw—but with two bishops, don't call it a draw, just think of them as your family, and you will win! The king can be mom or dad. Do you have a sibling? You and your brother or sister are the bishops.

About this activity

You are trying to trap the king in the corner. One bishop will give check, the other will prevent the king from escaping. Your king will also guard escape squares. Checkmate!

You can play by yourself or with a partner. One person is the king and the other is the king and two bishops. That's all you need, plus a board!

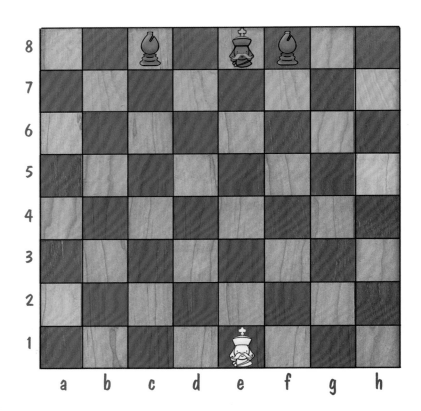

1 Set up your chessboard as above. (In a regular game, by the time we get to this point with everything else off the board, it is unlikely these pieces will be at their home squares! Nevertheless, you can force a checkmate from any position with a king and two bishops, so we'll start here for simplicity.)

2 Here's the idea: Big Brother (that's you, one of the bishops) wants to go outside and play, and of course your younger brother (the other bishop) wants to play, too. Your dad (the king) says, "Sure you can play, as long as I can play as well." So, it's important to keep everyone together! You will move the bishops and king forward, but keep them in a straight line. Play these moves out on your chessboard. The black team can go first in this game.

1. ... Bd6
2. Ke2 Be6
3. Kd3 Kf7
4. Ke4 Kf6

Your board should now look like this one.

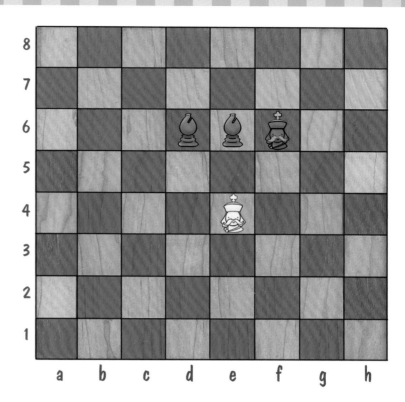

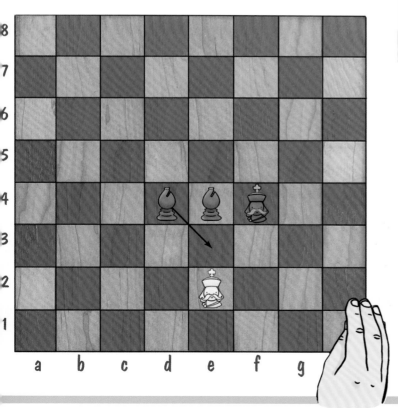

3 Everyone must huddle together, then all move forward. Don't leave anyone behind, and don't go off by yourself! Watch how the moves continue:

1 Kd4 Kf5 (When White moves the king to d4, we can't play Be5 without letting the white king escape from the "box" that you have created around him. So move your king to f5 instead.)

2. Ke3 Be5
3. Kd3 Bd5
4. Ke3 Be4
5. Ke2 Bd4
6. Kd2 Kf4
7. Ke2

What do you play now? Yes—Be3!

Notice how we are secretly creating a box around the white king by crisscrossing the bishops and filling any gap with the king? It may look more like a triangle, but these bishops work very well together.

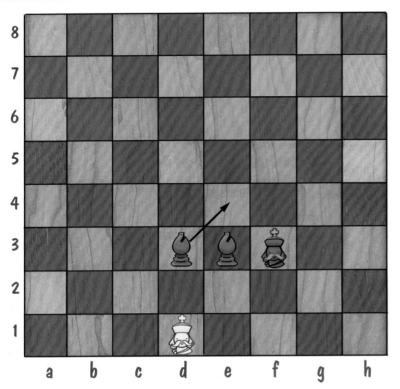

Continue with the following moves:
1. Kd1 Bd3
2. Ke1 Kf3
3. Kd1

Your family is still together in a line and has now trapped the king on the edge of the board.

Your job now is to try to get the king to go closest to your own king's corner. How can you do this? First, move your bishop to e4 — look how that traps the king. He can't go to c1 or d2 (they're guarded by the bishop on e3), he can't go to c2 (that's guarded by the bishop on e4), and he can't go to e2 (that's guarded by the king).

5

Once the white king moves to e1 (his only option), you can bring a bishop to c2 to prevent him running to a1 and force him ever closer to h1. When the white king continues to f1, push on with a bishop to d2, then create **opposition** (by moving the black king to g3) when the king reaches g1! This prevents the king from escaping to the second rank. Here are the moves:
1. Ke1 Bc2
2. Kf1 Bd2
3. Kg1 Kg3

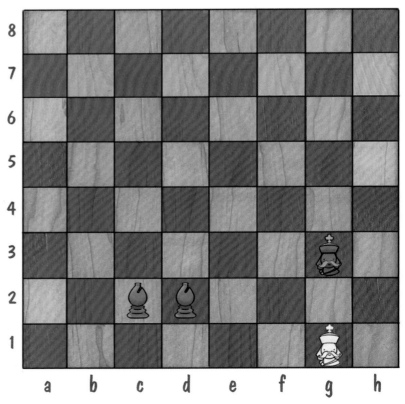

6 The white king doesn't want to move into the corner, but he can't go far—watch what happens in the following moves:

1. Kf1 Bd3+ (Check!)
2. Kg1

Your turn! It's mate in two… how can the bishops keep checking the king and force him into the corner? (There's a clue on the diagram, and the solution is at the bottom of the page.)

Fun fact

You cannot force a checkmate with only one bishop (nor with one knight or two knights). And if you only have two kings left on the board, that's also a draw.

Let's review!

1. Keep your family (the two bishops and king) together: huddle up, then spread out on the same line.

2. Trap the king on the edge of the board.

3. Find the corner closest to your king, and FORCE the opponent's king to that corner!

Solution to 6:
After the king moves to e3, your bishop moves to g1—it's check again. The king can't move anywhere, except to h1. Move your other bishop to e4—checkmate!

Blindfold Chess

In blindfold chess, you are not necessarily literally blindfolded, but you are unable to see the board and pieces while you play. Sounds crazy? It's definitely not easy, but it will absolutely help you with your visualization skills! Visualization is when you are trying to "see the board in your head." When you imagine what happens next, it is called "calculating." Playing blindfold chess will help you visualize and calculate! It's also good for your memory skills. See if your parents will play with you!

About this activity

This game is for three people—two players and one referee. The players say the moves they want to make, and the referee uses a hidden chessboard to make the moves, and ensure that they are legal. If someone makes an illegal move, the referee must stop play and announce that the move was illegal.

The referee will need a chessboard with letters and numbers on it, and one bag of chess pieces.

Try to play at least five moves (for each side) without making an illegal move.

1 Stare intently at the blank chessboard and imagine where all the pieces would be. Make your first move by announcing it clearly in chess notation. (This is why you should use a board with letters and numbers—it will be much easier to use notation!) The ref will make the move on the hidden board. Take turns.

For example, let's say you want to move the pawn in front of the king two squares. Say, "e4!" Try not to touch the board with your fingers—only use your visualization skills!

2 If you are capturing something, you should try to announce what it is you're capturing.

3 Call check when your opponent's king is in danger! If you can make it to three moves without accidentally capturing one of your own pieces or going through danger, consider it a success!

4 Try to get to five moves each, or more! When you have reached your limit (and I'd say start with only five moves!), the ref can ask if you and your partner can either replay the moves, or set up the current position (after your five moves were made). This is yet another challenge!

Next time you play, change roles, so that you each get a chance at being the referee as well as playing.

Variations

You can play this activity by yourself. Try to replay moves of a famous game, for example, in your head. You could use a chess book with famous games and instead of replaying them on a board, do the moves in your head only!

Why not try playing without any board at all? A third person should still help by making the moves on a real board, hidden from the other two players.

Progressive Chess ☺☺☺

Progressive chess is designed to help you plan ahead and develop an attacking attitude! You should be able to make a quick checkmate. The move count increases with each turn. So White goes first and gets one move; then Black goes and gets two moves in a row; then White gets three moves; Black gets four; and so on. The number increases by one each time until someone makes checkmate! This is usually achievable in fewer than ten moves of this game.

About this activity

Aside from the move counts increasing, there is one other rule in this game: if you make check, you lose the rest of your turns. That means that if you have ten moves, but you make check on move five, you don't get to make five more moves. Your opponent will have to escape immediately from check, but will still have all the rest of their moves (11 in total).

You'll need a regular chess set, with all the pieces in their starting positions, and a partner.

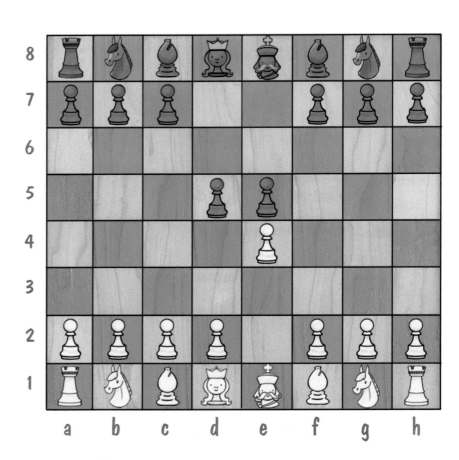

1

Here is an example game. White plays pawn to e4, then Black plays e5 and d5.

2 White now gets three moves in a row. Look carefully and see how you can win the queen with the bishop. You need three moves to do this—perfect! White moves d4, Bg5, and Bxd8.

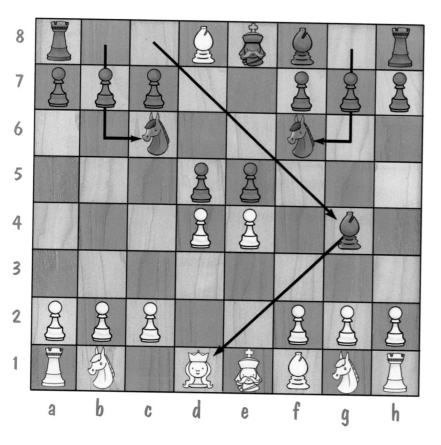

3 Black uses his four moves to counter by bringing out both knights, then prepares to take the queen back with the bishop. (In notation, that's Nc6, Nf6, Bg4, and Bxd1.)

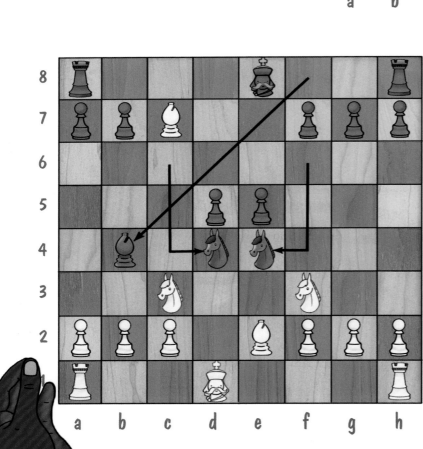

4 White plays five moves: Kxd1, Bxc7, Nc3, Nf3, and Be2.

5 White wasn't very careful with those moves—Black can crush! First, Black brings out her bishop and knights a bit closer to the king (Nxd4, Nxe4, Bb4). Can you find a mate-in-three in this position? Remember, Black has a total of six moves this time, so has three more moves to make. White is simply frozen.

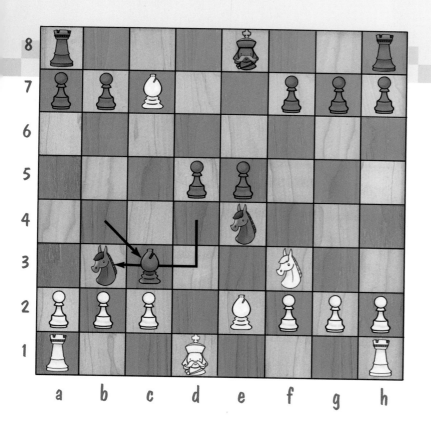

6 Black's next two moves are Nb3 and Bxc3—she has one more move to make. What should she do?

7 That's right: Black takes the pawn at f2 with her knight and it's checkmate! The knight that just moved is aiming at the king. The bishop on c3 is aiming at d2 and e1, so the king cannot move to either of those squares, and the knight on b3 is aiming at c1, so the king cannot move there either. Neither can White block (since you can never block a knight's check), nor capture the knight! No escape!

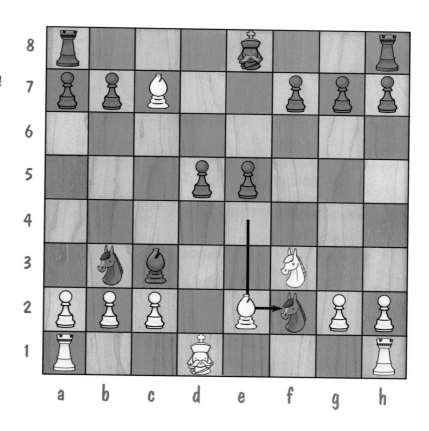

Deny!

Here you are going to have to try to trick your opponent into thinking your plan is one thing, when it's really another! You will also be trying to work out what your opponent's plan is. In this activity, when your opponent makes a move, if you don't like it, you can say, "Deny!" and they have to take it back! (Deny means that you do not allow something to happen; you could equally say "Take back!") You can do this only one time each move. Sounds great, huh? Except they can do the same to you, too...

About this activity

If you don't like your opponent's move, say "Deny!" and they'll have to choose something else! But if you do like it, do not say "Deny," and just play your own move.

There is a lot of psychology (how things in your mind affect the way that you play) that goes on in chess. This activity is all about having two plans at the same time. Your first plan may well be denied by your opponent, but that's why you have a second plan (remember that they can only deny you once each move).

Psychology comes in when your second plan is better than the first. Try to make your opponent think you're going with your first plan—when they deny you that one, you have the better one ready to go!

This game is for two players.

1 Checkmate is the goal, as always, but it is very hard to do! Think about it: if you make checkmate, your opponent is not going to like it! He or she will say "Deny!"—and you'll have to take it back.

So keep your checkmates "hidden," if you can. If you can make another move first and your opponent denies it—for example, if you capture one of their pieces, they probably won't like it and will tell you to take it back—then you could make checkmate, because they cannot say "Deny!" twice on one move!

Another way to win is if you have two ways to make checkmate. This is really brilliant because if they deny once, they cannot deny again!

DENY!

Top tip

In regular chess, there are no take backs! A computer game might let you, but in a professional game it's not allowed. That means you'll have to think differently from normal about this activity!

2 Start out by playing regular moves. Try 1. e4 e5 and 2. Nf3 Nc6. If White wants to mess up Black's opening, he can "deny" her a move he is used to playing, like Nc6, and Black will be forced to play a worse move.

Black would have to think of another way of guarding the pawn on e5… or would she? Actually, if White ever tries to capture it, Black could just deny him/her! (The only problem is if White has TWO possible captures; in that case, he will be able to make one of them happen!)

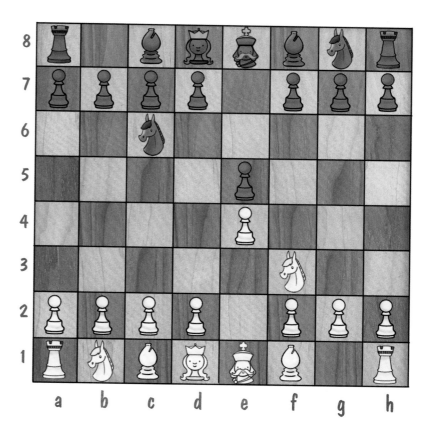

Musical Chess

Sometimes you win in chess, and sometimes you lose (and sometimes you get a draw...) but in this game, you could go from winning to losing when someone says the word "Switch!" In this game, you will practice perspective—the ability to see a game from both sides. We call it "musical chess" because it's like musical chairs—when "the music stops" (when the referee stops play), you have to switch places with your partner. When play starts again, you'll be playing as the opposite color!

About this activity

Perspective is important because it's good to remember that both sides are trying to win. You have your own plans and ideas, and your opponent has theirs. If you don't ask yourself, "What's the threat?" you may miss something big!

This game is for three people —two players and a referee. As always, checkmate wins!

1 Set up the chessboard and start playing a normal chess game with your partner. When the referee says "Switch!" you have to swap places! (You might want to put your chessboard on a rotating tray or turntable to spin the board around, instead of swapping places with your partner—but be careful that pieces don't move or fall as you turn the board around.)

2 There is some chess psychology going on in this game! When you have to switch sides with your partner, you will suddenly be playing with the opposite color, and the whole board will look different! You may have been attacking, and now you are defending. Or you may have been losing by a queen, and now you are up a queen! How calmly can you react to these different scenarios?

Variation

Play with a whole group of people! You'll still need a referee to say when to switch. It's helpful if you can set up everyone's tables in a row. Everyone plays their game at the same time (so if you have six people playing, you'll have three chess games in progress), but when the referee stops play, everyone moves one place to the right. The person at the end of the row would come around to the other side of the table.

The referee has to make sure that everyone knows whose turn it is on the board, so their announcement should be, "As soon as it's White turn, stop playing." That way, when everyone shifts to the right, they know it will be White's move next, no matter which board they sit at.

Top tip

The referee could use a timer to make sure that it's a fair game and there isn't too long or short a time between each stopping point.

Bughouse

This game is going to knock your socks off! With two boards set up side by side, you sit next to your partner and each play a game. Sounds normal so far, but every time you win a piece, you hand it to your partner to add to their game. Suddenly they could have three rooks or two queens! This game will help you to play more aggressively, since hanging back and waiting is NOT the best strategy. Forceful moves like checks are likely to win the game.

About this activity

This game requires two chess sets and two teams of two players (so four players in total). Both games start at the same time and continue running alongside each other. (Players do not need to make the same moves at the same times—they will all play at their own pace.) When you capture a piece, you hand it to your partner to use!

Sometimes a chess clock is set up so that no one stalls on their turn, but you don't have to use one.

The goal is checkmate! If you checkmate your opponent, you win, and your partner automatically stops playing because he/she's just won, too!

1 Set up the two chess sets side by side, but with opposite colors next to each other. You will sit next to your partner, who will then have the opposite color from you. (So if you are White, your partner has to play as Black.)

Start playing the two chess games at the same time. Each time you capture a piece, give it to your partner! That means your partner could amass a giant army of pieces, or place one as soon as it is handed over and it's his/her turn to move. At the same time, he/she is handing pieces to you (and your opponents are doing the same thing). You will totally get the hang of it once you start playing!

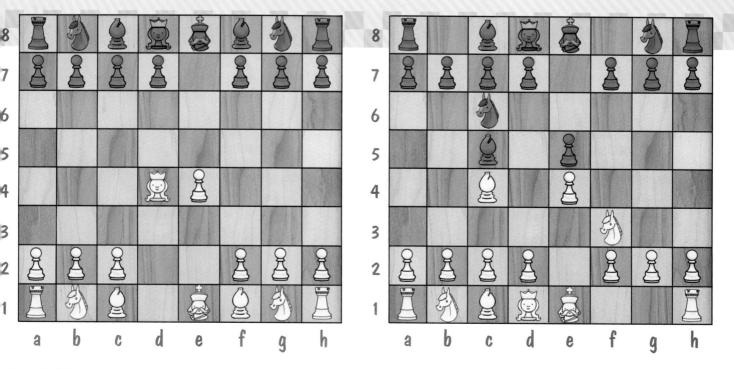

2

Let's look at an example game. On the left-hand board, Black and White have both just captured a pawn. The game has gone as follows:

1. e4 e5
2. d4 exd4
3. Qxd4

The right-hand board is the partner game, and it has gone slightly differently:

1. e4 e5
2. Nf3 Nc6
3. Bc4 Bc5

On this board, both White and Black now have an extra pawn to use! White might save hers, but, depending on what White does, Black might place the pawn on g4 on his next turn!

Top tip

Take advantage of weak squares like f2 and f7 immediately! Having control will be really helpful when you start adding pieces your partner has captured and given to you.

Bughouse rules

Some things you should know in this game:

- Placing a piece counts as your turn and can only be done on your turn. (So you could either place a piece or move a piece each turn.)

- You can place a piece anywhere you want, except on top of another piece. (That means you can place the king in check. And you can also place him in checkmate!)

- There is no "touch move rule" (see page 62) because pieces are going back and forth, left and right.

- Pawns are not allowed to be placed on the first or the very last ranks.

Solutions

King Travels page 54

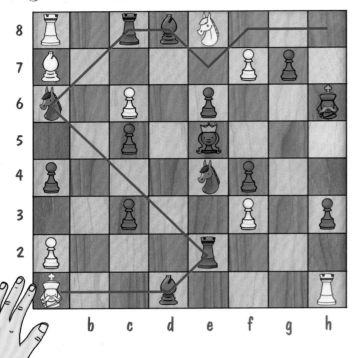

Trap the Queen, page 80

Solution to 5:
Bd1.

Solution to 6:
If Qxh1, Black plays Bc6, skewering the king to the queen. If the queen stays anywhere else on the first rank, the rook will simply capture her for free.
If Qc2, Bxc2.
If Qd3, Rh3 skewers.
If Qe4, Bc6 pins.
If Qf5, Rf1 skewers.
If Qg6, fxg6.
If 1. Qh7 Rxh5 2. Qxh5 Bd1 skewers, and if 2. Q moves anywhere else along the diagonal, the same pins/skewers exist. If she moves back to b1 then Rh1 traps her in the same way!
If 1. Qa2 Bb3 traps the queen because if 2. Qxb3 Rh3 skewers the king to the queen! An open board, and nowhere to go!

Scholar's Mate, page 86

Solution to variations:
Pawn to g6.

Create-a-Discovery, page 90

Solution to 6:
Black moves the rook down to e1, and then both he and the bishop give check to the king. This would be checkmate, because:
- the white rook may not capture the rook (since the bishop would still be giving a check)
- the white rook can't capture the bishop either (since the rook would still be giving a check)
- the king cannot move
- there is no way to block two checks
It's a discovered double check checkmate!

Resources

For further help and ideas, try the following resources:

ChessKid.com
www.chesskid.com
Loyds, The Queen Dance, Dog on the Loose!, and Double Bishops originated from articles written by Jessica E Prescott for the ChessKid website.

Over the Chessboard (author's website)
www.overthechessboard.com

How to Beat Your Dad at Chess by Murray Chandler (Gambit Publications)

Winning Chess Strategy for Kids by Jeff Coakley (Chess'n Math Association)

Play Like a Girl!: Tactics by 9Queens by Jennifer Shahade (Mongoose Press)

Bobby Fischer Teaches Chess by Bobby Fischer, Stuart Margulies, and Don Mosenfelder (Bantam)

The Chess Kid's Book of Checkmate by David MacEnulty (Random House)

Chess Camp series by Igor Sukhin (Mongoose Press)

All publications by Chess-in-the-Schools

Index

Acknowledgments

This has been an amazing project. Thank you to CICO Books for offering me this challenge to write a completely new type of chess book for kids. Carmel Edmonds and Robin Gurdon have been very thorough and thoughtful editors, and I think they can probably play a formidable game now.

Belated thanks to my parents, Jill and Jeff Martin, who taught me how to play when I was tiny, and then encouraged me to stick with it when all the other girls dropped off. To Ken Larsen who invited me to teach with him at my alma mater, and who introduced several of these chess variants to me when I was young.

Some of the original ideas for these activities came from brilliant colleagues at Chess-in-the-Schools. Elizabeth Vicary, Sean O'Hanlon, Ella Baron, Nathan Goldberg, and David MacEnulty, to name a few, are consistently doing amazing work with kids. A belated thank you to the late Steve Herx who encouraged me in those early years to: "Do what you can with what you have." Thanks to long-time friend Ian West for his sense of humor and availability in answering archaic questions.

Constant appreciation for my husband, Jason Prescott, who has changed his very fair share of diapers when I needed to work, and read and reread at any hour at my request.

There are those who have faith in you—what a wonderful gift. Thank you to Jill Martin, Jason Prescott, my parents-in-law Carol and Myron Prescott, Rabbi Barbara Thiede, and Danny Rensch of Chesskid.com, who have supported me as I've navigated the "working-mother" waters.